The Entrepreneurial Mom's Guide to RUNNING YOUR OWN BUSINESS

Kathryn Bechthold

Self-Counsel Press
(a division of)
International Self-Counsel Press Ltd.
Canada

Self-Counsel Press acknowledges the financial support of the Government of Canada through the Canada Book Fund (CBF) for our publishing activities.

Printed in Canada.

First edition: 2011

Library and Archives Canada Cataloguing in Publication

Bechthold, Kathryn

The entrepreneurial mom's guide to running your own business / Kathryn Bechthold.

ISBN 978-1-77040-059-7

1. New business enterprises.   2. Work and family.   3. Self-employed — Family relationships.   I. Title.

HD62.5.B42 2010   658'.041   C2010-902049-9

The author is grateful to many people for granting permission to quote them in this book. Thanks to Kajal Bahadur, Jennifer Broe, Amber Black, Kathy Buckworth, Sheil Caldwell, Ann Carlsen, Traci Costa, Esther Chung, Kim Duke, Erica Ehm, Betsy Fein, Julie Freedman Smith, Jessica Jacobs, Pegg Johnson, Michelle Kelsey, Michelle LaBrosse, Kim Lavine, Sharole Lawrence, Jaime Mann, Dr. Janet Miller, Christine Poirier, Crystal Reynolds, Lindsay Ross, Michelle Staley, Erica Swanson, Andrea Tumato, Jo-Ann Vacing, Jane Walter, and to the many others interviewed whose quotes were not used this time, and to those who wished to retain partial or complete anonymity.

Every effort has been made to obtain permission for quoted material. If there is an omission or error, the author and publisher would be grateful to be so informed.

Cover Image

Copyright©iStockphoto/Balancing children and work/Fertnig

Self-Counsel Press
(a division of)
International Self-Counsel Press Ltd.

1704 North State Street
Bellingham, WA 98225
USA

1481 Charlotte Road
North Vancouver, BC V7J 1H1
Canada

Contents

To my children, Charlotte and James,
who teach me on a daily basis what is really important in life.

To Derek, who has supported me through richer and poorer.

To my mother, who has taught me courage.

Acknowledgments

I would like to thank all of the women who participated in being interviewed for this book. Your genuine answers and compelling stories made this book an honest and real look at what being an entrepreneurial mom is like.

A special thanks to my assistant Tamara Schroeder, who successfully managed to source and interview the many women that have been featured in this book. To Kim Duke, Dr. Janet Miller, Esther S. Chung, Ann Carlsen, and Sylvia Daoust for their expertise and advice that have supported this book.

I would also like to thank my editor, Tanya Howe. It was a pleasure working with you.

Finally to my family who was patient while mommy went and wrote her book in the basement.

Notice to Readers

Laws are constantly changing. Every effort is made to keep this publication as current as possible. However, the author, the publisher, and the vendor of this book make no representations or warranties regarding the outcome or the use to which the information in this book is put and are not assuming any liability for any claims, losses, or damages arising out of the use of this book. The reader should not rely on the author or the publisher of this book for any professional advice. Please be sure that you have the most recent edition.

Introduction

"A better term for failure is feedback."

— Jesse Wilson

Mothers are born entrepreneurs. As soon as we become aware of our ability to create something as perfect and stupendous as children, it becomes very easy to dream of our next magnum opus.

I have owned a handful of businesses in my career — some great and some stinkers. What I find most extraordinary is how similar the themes of success are, whether you are running a babysitting business or a national magazine. What is even more extraordinary are the women who do it with small children underfoot. What I hope to accomplish with this book is to teach you about my mistakes and show you my successes, and introduce you to some other successful mothers in business so that you can learn from them as well. It takes a community to raise a child; the same goes for a new business.

As women, we are born community builders. My intention in being an entrepreneur has always been to build a network of strong women who have aligned priorities. My intention as a mother is to be the primary caregiver to my children, and to be the great mother that my mom taught me to be. I think this has been one of my most successful strategies at driving whatever business I am working on; the fact that my network of women is continuously growing and our intention, as a whole, is to share with each other as well as share similar values as mothers.

As the founding editor of *The MOMpreneur Magazine*, I had the opportunity to read almost every new small-business or women's interest book that came on the Canadian market — a lot of reading. What I found most disappointing was the fact that most authors were uncomfortable discussing their flops as well as their successes. It is when we are truly challenged and life becomes really difficult that the most important lessons are learned.

Did you know that you just bought a book on how to be successful as an entrepreneurial mom from a flop? Now before you run back to the store or try to figure out how to return this book to Amazon, let me reassure you that you will come away from this book with tools that will allow you to breathe easier and stand tall in times that test your resolve. The only way I know how to do that is to be truly honest about the challenges I have faced in my entrepreneurial career and to tell you how I have been successful while being the primary caregiver to my two children.

As I mentioned earlier, I am a true serial entrepreneur. The business I am most proud of today, however, is the one that seriously flopped — and I mean flopped with a capital F. My real passion for being entrepreneurial began while I was in university earning money on the side by working with children with severe neurological disabilities. For the most part, I worked with children with Autism Spectrum Disorder (ASD). By the time I graduated, I had earned some respect in the community as a woman who cared about these children and advocated for the families' rights in attaining funding from the provincial government. That client care, I believe, is what allowed my small consulting company to grow into an intervention agency that was 100 percent government funded as a provincial charitable organization within four years.

Unfortunately, being 100 percent government funded meant that I really only had one client; the government. There were no multiple streams of income to balance and stabilize my cash flow. Every decision made at the provincial level regarding these programs directly affected my business and yet was totally out of my control. Although it was some of the best work I have ever done, and some of the work that I am most proud of today, this business ended in a financial disaster that took years for me to recover from.

Although that failure was one of the most difficult times in my career and personal life, the lessons I learned from it have been some of the most important. When I look back at this company, I can now see certain key attributes that led to its failure. I am hoping these failures help you to understand your business better and how you can sustain your success for the long term.

Our first year of business was golden. We had cash in the bank, our incoming cash was flowing, clients were abundant, and my entire team and I were energized by the successes we were seeing in the treatment of our clients. We were able to see children learn everyday life skills such as communicating with others, playing with other children, and using the toilet — when other professionals had written them off as children who would never progress past the point of the developmental age of infancy. One of my most rewarding moments was seeing the mother of an eight-year-old child hear her son speak her name for the first time. As the population of newly diagnosed autistic children began to grow, the provincial agency that managed the funding for these programs began to restrict its spending in order to accommodate all children coming into that region.

When I look back, I see how our failure was inevitable from the beginning, although I certainly didn't see it then. Because I saw the tremendous growth opportunities available to the agency, I began to grow the charity aggressively. I signed a commercial lease for five years with a personal guarantee on the contract. I did not spend money at the strategic development level on consultation from a lawyer, an accountant, or professional fund-raisers — the equivalent of a professional sales team in the charitable sector. This would prove to be a terrible mistake.

Because our funding came directly from the provincial government, I did not invest in fund-raising for our charity outside of that stream of income. This would prove fatal as it ensured our reliance on one client and one client alone — the government. I clearly remember having a payroll of more than $50,000 every two weeks but only a few thousand dollars in my bank account. Despite an enormous accounts receivable, our income was just not reliable as far as timing.

As with most entrepreneurs, I scraped and clawed my way out of those situations, often personally supporting the payroll, always believing it would get better. What it ended up doing was driving me further and further into an untenable financial situation. As more and more children were diagnosed and came to the province for assistance, the provincial government had no choice but to start to take a look at how much funding was allotted per child in order to address the needs of all of the children pouring into the system. This is where the business really started to crumble. To compensate, I took more and more children on as clients in order to meet the needs of our miniscule budget.

As our cash flow became more restricted, I began to borrow small amounts because I believed that the work we were doing was such high quality that our program would continue to sustain itself and grow to new levels of success. I never thought our funding would be eliminated. I believed the good work we were doing would be recognized. In fact, the opposite happened.

As things became more stressful, it became more difficult to see outside my arena of hardship for a solution to break free of that sinking ship. When I look back, I think I was young and too naïve to believe it would ever completely sink, but sink it did and in a big way. Although I can now see its downward spiral over three years, I wasn't able to admit it until the bitter end, up to my eyeballs in debt, having borrowed from the bank, my parents, and through my credit cards — if there was money available, I used it on the company. We finally closed our doors on September 24, 2004, eight weeks after my wedding — you can only imagine what my mother-in-law thought! I still find it hard to believe that a service that was so popular and had a waiting list was not able to sustain itself. I now realize it was because of my choices that it failed — a bitter pill to swallow.

Since this experience, I have learned that when you begin your career as an entrepreneur, what you don't want to recognize is that your first business is often (and statistically proven to be) a dress rehearsal for the next and more profitable endeavors to come. Failures, although upsetting and stressful, are often a fact of life that you must prepare for and see as a stepping stone to your next career achievement. What I want to teach you is how to avoid the enormous failures and losses in your career and make you nimble enough to react and change early enough to sidestep a failure.

Once the loss of that business sunk in, I fell into a deep depression. What I didn't know at the time was that the loss of that business would teach me some of the best skills going forward — and it would be a far better teacher than any university or high-paid consultant ever would be. I knew I had to move on, but felt enormous shame and embarrassment because something I had put so many years into and had sacrificed so much for did not pan out. At the time the business shut its doors, I was newly married and definitely feeling like a failure. I decided to get pregnant in order to move on. I know, I know — those of you who have children are laughing at how ludicrous the idea of having a baby to move on from a depression is, but I swear, I think the sex was helpful!

Since having my daughter, I realize that I may not be the only woman out there who has chosen pregnancy in order to move on from a difficult time in her life. I have always wanted children, even more so once I was married, but looking back, I wish I had chosen to have her just for her and not as a distraction from other pain. What I learned about depression is that it doesn't go away on its own, and adding a pregnancy doesn't make it better. In fact, it makes it much, much worse.

Once my daughter was born, our money was totally gone. I had gone bankrupt nine months earlier and I had one year of a small maternity leave benefit to figure out what I was going to do next and how I was going to contribute to our family financially. My husband was monitoring every penny we spent and continuously bringing up the question of when I would go back to work. He even suggested I get a job driving a school bus with my daughter in tow. Not that there is anything wrong with that job, but I had built a million-dollar-a-year charity with more than 50 staff. I knew my potential was greater but I did not know how to get there.

The pressure was enormous; the depression I had suffered from earlier morphed into a beast called postpartum depression and intense anxiety that went undiagnosed for the next year. It would not be until I started working again that I would begin to feel less anxious and more in control of my future. My anxiety at going back to work was crushing. I felt a burning shame at the thought of running into one of my old colleagues, and I was overwrought with worry that we would never be financially stable again. My husband was resentful that he was the only breadwinner, and that I was not showing much interest in getting a job. Needless to say, it was a difficult time.

However, I loved every moment of being with my daughter, even the moments when I thought I would drop dead from sleep deprivation, sore nipples, and overall exhaustion. But, we needed money, and I needed to work. Out of pure desperation to bring some money in, I began writing business plans about any business I had ever considered and could do from home with my daughter in tow. It was a wild and exciting time as I truly felt that my options were limitless. My husband was happy to see me back on my feet and therefore really supportive of another venture (as long as it brought some money in). I had a beautiful, healthy daughter who, luckily, napped regularly and was genuinely happy to truck around the city researching business ideas. I began to build a network of people who were supportive of me finding a new passion.

I wrote about everything I thought might be profitable. I was interested in baking so I looked into a cake shop. I was interested in writing and reading new novels so I looked into becoming a literary agent. I felt I had some experience with fund-raising and grant writing from my charitable background so I looked into consulting in the nonprofit sector. It was an exciting time because I began to see a way out of the mess I had created and I was learning how to recognize a successful business model versus a broken one. I quickly began to recognize how much money I would need to invest in order to turn a profit from carefully calculated cash flows of my first year and I took very conservative looks at how I would sell different products or services in order to meet my family's financial needs.

It was important for me that my business met certain achievable goals. The following were my targets that the business I chose would have to reach:

- It would have to be something that allowed me to work from home with my daughter and bring me an income of $1,500 per month. That was what I needed in order to make my budget work. (My husband still laughs at how little money I needed then.)

- It needed to have a very low start-up investment. I took $10,000 from my home equity (I was thankful for the housing boom in my area) to start my next business and it couldn't cost more than that amount; otherwise, it would be cat-food stew for dinner.

- Because of my lack of start-up funds, it needed to be a business that I could do mainly by myself, at least until the business could sustain employees or contractors. My only staff support was still breast-feeding and preferred watching *The Wiggles*!

- It had to be something that I truly enjoyed because I knew how much emotional, physical, and financial investment it would take. I was still up with my daughter at night (first baby, didn't have the heart to "Ferberize" her yet) and I knew I would have to love what I was doing to stay conscious throughout the sales cycle.

From this list and from my list of business plan drafts, The Mompreneurs Networking Group Inc. was born. It had everything on my list and more. It allowed me to connect to a group of women (i.e., potential buyers and friends) and facilitate the growth of a new and blossoming community in the Canadian market — a community that continues to grow and develop today. From this business, I learned so much more, including —

- lessons learned from other entrepreneurial moms;

- how to build a website and how to update it;

- how to network;

- how to use social media marketing;

- how to sell;
- how to speak in front of a group;
- how to address my market via TV, the Web, and radio;
- how to negotiate a Unanimous Shareholders Agreement with professional investors; and
- how to sell my business.

My most important achievement has been that I was able to do this while being the main caregiver of my children. This has been my real accomplishment as I look back on my businesses over the last 15 years.

1. Why Are You Reading This Book?

I decided to write this book for three different groups of women:

- The women who continue to believe that their business is their "baby" and have their identities so wrapped up in it that they cannot see when it is broken.
- The women who want to become work-at-home entrepreneurs while being the primary caregiver to their children.
- The women who have businesses that are leaving the infancy stage and need a new set of lessons in order to move forward to a more sustainable business model.

For the last decade, women in North America have quickly surpassed men in starting new businesses. It is an economic reality that full-time childcare is difficult to find, expensive, and for many women, not their ideal choice going forward. Although corporations are still trying to figure out how to keep professional women after they have children, working 80-plus hours a week for someone else while not being able to be with your kids lacks a certain appeal.

Since the loss of the charity I founded, a real pet peeve of mine has been women who refer to their businesses as their "babies." What I want to emphasize is that while your business is something you should be passionate about, it should be a vehicle to making you money and leveraging your career. If it does not, then you have basically built yourself a very expensive hobby that will eventually suck you dry. You have to learn to evaluate your business on a monthly basis so that you can properly discern whether or not it is achieving your goals. If it is not, you need to learn to fix it now or cut it loose and move on before it overtakes you.

Now, I know that the last time your four-year-old smeared peanut butter across your new cashmere sweater or barfed on your latest financial statements you considered selling that child to the nearest nomadic clan, but I also know you got over it and remembered how sweet he or she really is once the child is asleep for the day and looking like his or her old cherubic self! What I want you to be able to do is to quickly assess whether or not your business model is broken, fix it, and recognize that if it is not fixable, you need to either walk away or sell it — fast. This is not something we would do with our babies, but you have to be ruthless and more practical as an entrepreneur. We are here to make money — priority number one when it comes to working — let's not compare this with our children. We also need to recognize that we are more than our businesses. Businesses will come and go; we need to be secure in ourselves, and tough enough to say what needs to be said in order to not go down with a sinking ship like I did.

For the women who are interested in leaving the corporate lifestyle and becoming an entrepreneurial mom, congratulations! This is going to be one of the most fun, chaotic, and exhilarating times of your life and you get to do it on your own terms! What is most important for you is to know what your terms are. Is it a set amount of income each month? Being the primary caregiver to your children? Achieving a certain amount of clients? Or manufacturing a certain amount of product? You must know each of these key targets and have them embedded into your business plan in order to know where you are going and plan for how you are going to get there.

For the women who have had a business for a few years and need a new injection of inspiration and some new skills, I hope this book will be the vehicle to provide that to you. I have included interviews with other successful women in business in the book as well; I hope you find them as inspiring as I have.

If you are feeling a bit lost in where your business is going, the following are some questions I want you to start asking yourself. If you answer no to the following questions, I still want you to read this book because I have been there, too. In fact, I have learned that balance is not really achievable. To quote Julie Freedman Smith, "What we need to find is harmony in our day and profit in our businesses."

1.1 Am I taking any money as a salary?

This is a tough one, as it does take some time to make a business into a profitable return on investment, but at what point do you have an opportunity and at what point is it no longer viable to continue along the same path? You need to know what these two points are clearly and concisely and then you need to have the guts to act on them. You need to learn to become flexible enough to change the plan when it no longer works and start fresh. Follow the money. Learning to acknowledge, sooner rather than later, that the business model is broken, will save you a lot of time and a tremendous amount of cash — not to mention your relationships.

1.2 Am I spending time growing my business to become more profitable?

What do you spend the most amount of your time doing? Is it sales or is it answering emails and organizing your space? Everything is important but nothing surpasses cash flow. You always need to focus on profitability and growing those opportunities. If 80 percent of your revenue comes from 10 percent of your product or services, you need to revamp that business plan to follow the money.

1.3 Am I energized by what I am doing?

Are you a couple of years in and dread going into your office or answering the phone? Stop now. Don't waste any more time on what you are doing. Revamp your plan, start fresh, or walk away.

Every moment at work is time away from my kids — time I will never get back. If I don't love it then I have committed to myself that I will change it or get out.

1.4 Am I properly balancing home and work life?

How much time did you plan to spend on work when you started this project? How much time did you plan on spending away from your kids? Are you achieving these goals? I look back at my daughter's baby pictures and realize that through the fog of sleep deprivation and the distraction of difficult breast-feeding and hemorrhoids, I don't remember a lot from her first year. The time went by so fast. When my kids have moved away and are starting their own families, I can work like a dog. Now, I want to be a good mom, a really good mom, and build amazing memories that last along with my c-section scars, the tiger stripes on my belly, and dribble of pee that runs down my leg every time I sneeze.

1.5 Do I remember to act reasonably when I discipline my children?

Do I act reasonably when I discipline my children or am I so stressed out that I scream like a banshee when they play "how far can my booger fly"? As a kid, you always see those moments when your mom and your friends' moms lose it and fly off the handle. Whether it was you picking your nose in church or when your friends festively planted salami in your Christmas tree on your 14th birthday, there are times when all moms morph instantaneously into something out of *The Exorcist*. I have found a direct correlation between my work becoming too busy and me flying off the handle. Although sometimes warranted, I want to make sure when I fly off the handle it is for the right reasons and not because I haven't set appropriate boundaries for myself in my work.

1.6 Do I get much time to invest in my marriage or relationships outside of my business?

When my first business went down the toilet, there was not only a path of financial destruction but emotional loss as well. My business had become so totally a part of me that I had not built new friendships outside of work. My friends were those I worked with — those that were really angry when their paychecks evaporated. It was a horrific situation and difficult still to write about years later, but is also an important lesson I keep to this day.

2. How to Use This Book

"Money, if it does not bring you happiness, will at least help you be miserable in comfort."

— Helen Gurley Brown

Because I believe that women, especially entrepreneurial moms, need to stick together and support each other in order to become successful, I have tried to provide you with the most accurate and up-to-date information on how to be profitable in business in this book. I have detailed my worst experiences, and interviewed more than 150 entrepreneurial moms across North America to provide you with an objective idea of what it is really like, what to do, and what to avoid. I have also included some of my blog entries on my day-to-day entrepreneurial mom experiences that you can probably relate to. As well, I have included expert advice from lawyers, accountants, bookkeepers, and psychologists to give you a head start.

The CD includes many handy forms, such as a cash-flow worksheet and an employee evaluation form to name a few. The forms will help you stay organized and on track with your business. My website, www.entrepreneurialmombook.com, also offers items of use to entrepreneurs.

A New Economic Reality — Entrepreneurial Mothers

"Fed up with a corporate world that penalizes them for being both women and mothers, and gender inequities that are getting worse, women are beginning to take control of their financial destinies in record numbers by starting their own businesses."

— Kim Lavine, *The Mommy Manifesto*,
(New Jersey: Wiley, 2009).

There are nearly 11 million woman-owned companies in the US, 48 percent of all US businesses, and by 2025 the Census Bureau projects 55 percent of US businesses will be owned by women.[1]

I live in Canada, and although we have a one-year maternity leave, which is much longer than many countries including the US with its average six-week maternity leave, many women feel that returning to their corporate careers no longer fits with their priorities as a new Mama.

---

[1] Kim Lavine, *Mommy Millionaire*, (New York: St. Martin's Griffin, 2008).

Although corporations are quickly trying to figure out how to keep their highly educated and trained female employees once these women have children, many are failing at coming up with new and creative ways to develop their working environments to suit the needs of these women. Women today understand the pressures of careers and the dedication their careers need. It becomes clear very quickly that if they are going to work that hard and be separated from their families for that many hours per day, they might as well start to consider doing it on their own terms and for themselves.

Women in Canada are still far from reaching equality in the workplace. Even as I write this book, the national news is reporting that a new study has found that female professors still make far less money than their male counterparts in Canadian universities, and it doesn't get any better anywhere else:

- Earning differentials still hover around 30 percent between women and their male colleagues according to the Organisation for Economic Co-operation and Development (OECD).

- In Canada, approximately two-thirds of both male and female executives (67 percent of men and 64 percent of women) believe that gender equality in the workplace has improved in the last ten years. However, only one-third (32 percent) of all Canadian executives surveyed believe that men and women have equal opportunities in the workplace, and one-third (34 percent) of female executives in Canada believe that their gender limits their career opportunities, according to a recent study done by Accenture on the "thickness of the glass ceiling in North America."[2]

Appropriate childcare is another reason why so many women are leaving their corporate careers to establish their own businesses. Where I live, daycares often have waiting lists that begin at conception — I'm not kidding. When you get that blue line on the pee stick, you can then get your name on a childcare waiting list for baby's first birthday. Not only is it hard to find appropriate placements in a convenient time frame, the cost is exorbitant. Many North Americans can expect to pay upwards of 50 percent of their income to childcare costs. You can see how working from home has become more attractive.

If you do find a great, loving placement for your little ones, and you do have the kind of high paying career that allows you the luxury

2 Sarah Thompson, "Most Executives Believe Workplace Equality for Women Still Lags Behind Men, Accenture Study Shows," www.accenture.com, (2006), accessed 2010.

of affording childcare and your cost of living expenses, you will most likely have to work a crazy amount of hours in order to maintain your positive performance appraisals at work. Once your kids start their extracurricular activities — ballet, soccer, hockey, and violin lessons — you are running your daily life so fast that you can quickly forget about any quality of life, let alone little things like remembering to brush your teeth in the morning.

Now don't get me wrong, choosing to own your own business is no cake walk. You need to prepare for long hours, financial investment, busy schedules, and stress — but isn't it better to do that on your own schedule, work with clients you love, and take away the profit rather than handing that off to your boss?

"When I was on maternity leave with my fourth child, my nanny quit. I was working as a director of marketing at a large bank, and it had been quite a challenge juggling working full time with three children. So I decided this was a message to change things up, and I had also written my first book (THE SECRET LIFE OF SUPERMOM: HOW THE WOMAN WHO DOES IT ALL … DOES IT!) during that year-long maternity leave. I hung up the briefcase, picked up the pen, and never looked back. Now, five books later, as well as having had the opportunity to write for many magazines, be a frequent television and radio host/speaker, and work with corporations as a spokesperson to the mom market, I'm working harder than ever. But the positive side is that it's extremely flexible — my kids are now 8, 11, 17, and 19 — and with technology I'm able to carry a virtual office with me everywhere. I love it."

— Kathy Buckworth, author

"It is no great revelation that women have run the organization that has been the backbone of this country for generations — The FAMILY! If you study this organization that we call 'the family,' you will note it has been full of restructuring and downsizing over the years. It has been through a lot of cultural changes, but one of the constants has been the matriarch and her feminine leadership. Women are emerging as leaders of corporations, small businesses, educational institutions, and nonprofit organizations … To most women, these highly desirable management skills are second nature because they do all these things all the time at home, running the family organization, without even really thinking about it."

— Michelle Yozzo Drake,
From the Kitchen to the Corner Office:
Mom's Wisdom on Leadership,
(New York: Morgan James Publishing, LLC, 2008).

1. Motherhood: Reclaiming the Title and Living the Dream

"If you bungle raising your children, I don't think whatever else you do matters very much."

— Jackie Kennedy

I started *The MOMpreneur Magazine* when my daughter was four months old. By the time the business was really taking off, she was becoming more independent and could hang out with Daddy in the evenings. Having a second child while running a national magazine led to challenges. I distinctly remember a heated discussion with my board of directors while breast-feeding my son. There are times when I feel that every client of mine has seen my nipples more often than I have in the last year. Although that isn't always comfortable, I do feel good about the time I am getting to spend with my son, and I know that because I don't apologize for him being with me, he is readily accepted by the stakeholders in my business life.

"Being a mommy entrepreneur is a lot like being Ginger Rogers; doing everything Fred Astaire did, but 'backwards in high-heels,' while making it look effortless. My workday as President of Green Daisy, Inc., is routinely interrupted by numerous requests from my kids including 'can I have chocolate milk?' to 'can I buy a BB gun?' And you know what? That's a good thing! Seeing my children's smiling faces throughout the workday is one of the perks of being a Mommy Millionaire."

— Kim Lavine, *Mommy Millionaire,*
(New York: St. Martin's Griffin, 2008).

I have made decisions to slow down and change a few of my roles so that they interfere less in the first year of my son's life. It isn't always easy to make that transition and to trust others with your business opportunities, but you must in order to stay true to your priorities — not to mention giving your staff the space to breathe and to fall into a more superior role.

Choosing to be an entrepreneurial mom is no walk in the park; you have to be strong enough to draw boundaries around your family and ambitious enough to be profitable. The following are points to remember:

- ♥ You did this to have more control over your time and your family's time, don't blow it by losing sight of this goal.

- ♥ Have the guts to breast-feed your baby in a business meeting or do what you need to do when it comes to your children — you are a mom first. Stop apologizing for the toddler in the background having a potty break or the infant who just burped into the phone. You are a mompreneur and your children come first. Your business is what makes you money and allows you to be creative and keep your brain wet while your children grow. You can do both but you need to defend your boundaries like the "mama bear" you are.

- ♥ You must be strong enough to put in boundaries where your family is concerned. You must learn to recognize the best places to spend your time and evaluate every meeting, opportunity, and sales acquisition based on the dollar value it provides. If it doesn't build your business or your bank account, why are you spending that time away from your family?

2. Defining Success

The one commonality among the women I have interviewed for this book is that they all define success in business differently than someone that does not have to balance being the primary caregiver to their children. Success becomes primarily defined as being able to balance a lifestyle of raising a family and achieving career development.

While I owned *The MOMpreneur Magazine*, we found that 60 percent of self-employed women can be described as "lifestylers," meaning business owners who are not actively looking for growth opportunities, but are looking for ways to balance work and family needs.

Success is different for every mom I interviewed, but the bottom line of being a good mom never changes. Being a good mom was a trait desired 100 percent consistently for each of these women. Whether it is bringing in enough money to be the primary caregiver or if it is to surpass one million dollars in revenue next year, know your definition of success now. Have it clearly laid out, and focus on achieving it.

"Of course I would do it all again! I have learned some invaluable lessons that could only have been from freelancing. Depending on myself has shown me an inner strength and confidence I wouldn't have known about myself without my business. Knowing I can succeed all on my own on my terms is a huge step towards living the life I want."

— Crystal Reynolds, Crystal Ink Graphic Design

Business Planning

"When you start a business, there are so many things that can come up. I think I would have been better prepared to deal with some of the surprises if I had spent more time on my business plan."

— Jaime Mann, Lavish Lamb

No matter what business you choose, you need to plan in order to be successful. For me, I really wanted to start a magazine. I had no background in magazine production, I had never written professionally, and I had never advertised a business or looked too closely at advertising as a revenue stream. What I was interested in was the growing trend for women to leave the workforce to have children and to start businesses, instead of going back to the corporate world. One of my faults, and I would argue one of my assets, is my arrogance. I remember saying to my husband, "How hard could it be?" Little did I know, it would grow into something much more complex; but it did start simply.

I purchased the Adobe Creative Suite from the grocery store, then drove to my local bookstore to purchase *The Adobe Creative Suite All-in-One Desk Reference for Dummies* to do the layout of the magazine. I had a girlfriend walk me through developing a website from a template on Dreamweaver on the phone and I started calling businesses that regularly advertised in magazines to tell them about the concept of *The MOMpreneur Magazine*.

When I printed the first issue, it was not beautiful, and it did not look especially slick or professional. In fact, when I look at it now, it was downright ugly. My website even had a small letter "d" in the top right-hand corner and, for the life of me, I could not figure out how to get rid of it. For the first year of my business, I was regularly asked what the special meaning behind that "d" was. I wish I knew!

Despite all of this, what the magazine did have was great articles and honest content on how hard it was to balance a business with a new family — a message most women had an emotional reaction to because they were living it! It also had the feel of sitting down with a great girlfriend and being completely honest about the life of a mompreneur, something that included everything from business, to parenting, to sex. The word "mompreneur" evoked an extremely strong emotional reaction in people. They either hated it or they loved it — it didn't matter because they remembered it.

1. Making the Business Profitable

I attend many different events a week promoting women in business, and I never cease to be amazed at the creative ideas people have and turn into businesses. I am happy to wander by, appreciate, and move forward.

When I look at many different "virgin entrepreneurs" or people just stepping into their first businesses, I often see a microbusiness with no real profitability potential. When asked to give advice on the business, I always ask how much their revenue was in the prior year. That is where I start to hear a lot about passion, creativity, and dreams, blah, blah, blah. I love that these people have found their passion, have used their creativity to bring something to the marketplace, but without sales (and a lot of them), many of these will just be another business that has fallen in the "Oops, I created an expensive hobby instead of a business" category.

It is all fine and good to create a business that you love and want to invest your passion in, but do *not* do it if you cannot make it profitable. If you cannot lay out your cash-flow plan, identify how much you will need to sell, and know that you can sell it, don't do it. If you can't see anyone else in the marketplace succeeding in a business like yours, there is a reason why. Owning a business is expensive in its first years, therefore you might as well throw your money into the wind if you can't build a business plan based on a model that is proven.

From a business point of view, there are so many reasons to plan for success and have your direction clearly laid out. Yet, so many entrepreneurs continue to ignore this process, mostly because it is time consuming and can be boring if you don't know what you are doing and don't have some guidance on how to get it done. From an emotional perspective, this process has benefits as well.

Dr. Janet Miller, psychologist, offered the following advice:

"In business we want to have some kind of success, reach a financial goal, be recognizable, win an award, or reach a particular sales target … perhaps you are also interested in fulfillment, in making a difference, in creating a legacy, or in helping others … I think of these larger things as 'vision' — rather than goals — and I think that having vision is essential, be it in our professional lives, or our personal ones. Vision, for me, reflects what I stand for, who I am (or who I am becoming), it represents my future — my purpose perhaps, or my direction in life … it might be less tangible — not measured by outcomes, but more by feelings or by my sense of satisfaction …

Vision and goals are interrelated but distinct. Goals are short term, specific, outcome-related, and/or measurable, while visions tend to be more long term, global, less specific (more 'big picture'), and either not 'measurable' or perhaps measurable by a subjective scale (for example, a sense of feeling or accomplishment). We often need both goals and a vision to be successful.

Is it essential to have vision or goals? No. Sometimes we start out without a goal, or without a clear vision. This is okay; this might be our way of beginning — taking random steps, saying yes to everything for a while to see what fits us best, being open to what lies ahead, taking up unrelated activities or interests, going to school for a relatively random or varied set of courses — but at some point, most of us begin to define a goal (to get a degree, to find a job, to start a business, to move, etc.). Once we start to define goals, we often link to some kind of future vision — and then as that vision takes shape it will in turn inspire us to take on specific tasks with specific goals in mind. It's a chain reaction — and once it's in motion, it's often fairly easy to keep it going."

From the perspective of an entrepreneurial mom who has seen success as well as failure, business planning is essential. In my earlier years as an entrepreneur, when I chose to just "wing it," I was undisciplined in my spending, grew the business too fast, and could not keep up with customer service. I often experienced much more stress and anxiety than I needed to. If I had taken the time to know where I was going, how I was going to get there, and who I would need to help, I would have known sooner if it was going to be successful or not because I would have been able to compare it to my plan.

> "When I come in the office in the morning, I have a look at my agenda then scan my emails. I believe that making lists and setting priorities is important. It is very easy to get overloaded with little details or to spend too much time on things that are useless to the general objectives of the business (but so much fun to do). I ask myself the same questions that I would ask when managing money expenses at home. 'Do I really need this?' becomes 'Do I really need to do this?' or 'Should I keep my time for something else?' Every six months, I take the business plan out of the file cabinet and make sure that I am on the right track. It really helps to keep the big picture in mind."
>
> — Christine Poirier, Momzelle

Going forward, when I did have a business plan, I acquired funding much easier with banks because they saw me as a professional who was taking their investment seriously. As well, when I was approached by a potential investor, I was immediately ready for the meeting with my business plans and financial documents in order. That not only impressed them but allowed me to stand out from the crowd of other microbusinesses they approached.

> "I read a few books before starting work on the business plan. Those helped me crystallize my ideas. The original purpose of the business plan was to apply for a loan from the Canadian Youth Business Foundation, so we followed a format they laid out for us. We attempted a lot of market research but since we are dealing with two emerging industries — cloth diapers and slings — there was next to no information available. We did conduct a SurveyMonkey survey with our target market to determine our best options for things like what to carry and our potential location, as well as to show potential investors that interest in our niche existed. The business plan also included growth projections (conservative), information on our competitors, marketing plans,

a list of suppliers/products, and plans for things like hours, employees, and so on. I generally worked on the business plan about five hours per day, five days per week, for probably six to eight months.

The business plan has been essential in applying for loans and retail locations, but it also helped us to determine our game plan and examine areas we may not have considered."

— Lindsay Ross, Babes in Arms

2. Components of Your Business Plan

Writing a business plan is the single most important planning piece for a successful business. Without it, you might as well not even start because you won't know where you are going, how you are going to get there, and how much it will cost you, let alone how much you will make.

Every business plan needs to include the following components:

- **Executive summary:** A brief summary of your business, your goals, and what you need to achieve those goals.

- **Mission, vision, and values statements:** What your main goals are and how you are going to achieve them.

- **Corporate structure:** How you will set up your business (i.e., incorporation, sole proprietorship, partnership, etc.).

- **Company history:** This section includes a brief history of the company so far (i.e., steps you have taken, achievements, and failures).

- **Product pricing:** What your pricing strategy consists of.

- **Target market analysis:** Who the target market is, how much money they make, what they do for careers, how educated they are, their lifestyles, their families — everything you can think of, or have asked them about in a survey.

- **Competitor analysis:** Analyze what percentage of the market share you competitors own, how they get it, what they are doing well, and what can you do better. Describe what makes your business unique compared to your competitors.

- **Industry analysis:** Usually found in government statistics sites, the industry analysis gives you access to information on the industry you are in or are entering.

- ❦ **Management plan:** Who you will need to hire to make your business work.

- ❦ **Strategic alliances:** Who you can partner with to achieve your goals.

- ❦ **Marketing strategies:** What you will do to target your market and take the largest market share.

- ❦ **Production process:** What needs to happen to provide your service or manufacture your product.

- ❦ **Distribution strategies:** Distribution is one of the biggest challenges, so you will need to decide how you will get your product into the hands of your client.

- ❦ **SWOT analysis:** Analyze your strengths, weaknesses, opportunities, and threats.

- ❦ **Operations plan:** How the day-to-day operations will be run.

- ❦ **Financial plan:**
  - Balance sheet
  - Income statement
  - Cash-flow summary
  - Five-year projections

2.1 Executive summary

An executive summary is the component that includes an overview of everything you will be discussing in your business plan. It will include your mission statement and vision statement as well as what your product is, how you will sell it, who will sell it, and how you will make it. Many, including myself, prefer to write this piece last, summarizing the key features in each of the components you have written up until that point.

2.2 Mission, vision, and values statements

A mission statement is what defines your organization's purpose, quickly and concisely. A vision statement also guides your organization's direction and purpose but looks less at your bottom line and more at how you will achieve those goals based on your value systems.

When you begin your business, you need to have a firm grasp on your mission and vision statements. These key pieces are often pushed aside because of their supposed simplicity. Most people think they know their mission statement but in reality they do not have it honed enough to use professionally. I encourage you to specifically define what it is you are trying to accomplish. I always find it inspiring to look at models from successful businesses so I have included a few here:

Disney's mission statement:

The mission of The Walt Disney Company is to be one of the world's leading producers and providers of entertainment and information. Using our portfolio of brands to differentiate our content, services, and consumer products, we seek to develop the most creative, innovative, and profitable entertainment experiences and related products in the world.

McDonald's vision statement:

McDonald's vision is to be the world's best quick service restaurant experience. Being the best means providing outstanding quality, service, cleanliness, and value, so that we make every customer in every restaurant smile.

Disney and McDonald's statements provide a broad but clearly defined direction of where their companies are trying to go and what they are trying to achieve.

For the MOMpreneur, I produced the following mission statement:

The MOMpreneur® Networking Group Inc. strives to challenge women to plan to build large, influential, and successful companies. We endeavor to engage women to provide encouragement and leadership to be more successful in business and motherhood. We create an environment where women can learn from each other on how to innovate, be creative, and become more profitable. We challenge these women to choose excellence in what they do and to build strategic alliances in order to achieve success in their goals.

The vision statement for MOMpreneur was as follows:

The vision of The Mompreneur® Networking Group Inc. is to build a community of successful women by offering information, inspiration, education, and opportunities to enhance their businesses.

Later we developed a values statement:

The following values capture the essence of our commitment to the readers, contributors, advertisers, and stakeholders of our company which has been developed for and dedicated to women who are balancing the roles of motherhood and entrepreneurship. We uphold the family, support ambition, provide inspiration, and emphasize balance in all that we do.

We went on to talk about respect, innovation, integrity, financial independence, and harmony. Having this very specific definition allowed me and my team a structure under which to work. It became a real tool for me, on how to make my decisions for growth as well as day-to-day operations, not only from a profitability perspective, but from the perspective of matching our core values as mothers.

> "Initially I started Little Soles Inc. because I wanted to create a job for myself that would allow me the opportunity to work from home after my kids were born, allowing me to be around and involved more than if I was working away from the home. I wanted a job that would give me a creative outlet as well as create some income for myself.
>
> However, the movement and motivation behind Little Soles Inc. has changed greatly since its conception in 2005. Little Soles Inc. stands for so much more than just a job! Currently the goal of Little Soles® Footwear is to be an industry leader in the infant footwear sector, providing foot healthy, toxin free, environmentally conscious footwear. Now Little Soles Inc. has become a mission. A vehicle to which I can make a difference in the industry I so desperately wanted to be a part of."
>
> — Jessica Jacobs, Little Soles Inc.

2.3 Corporate structure

Once your basic values and statements have been put in place, you need to take a look at the corporate structure and how you want to conduct your business. My preference is to always incorporate a company to separate it as its own individual entity. Most importantly, this protects my personal assets from the liabilities of the company (in most cases). Some accountants will disagree with me on this in the early years because it does increase costs and reporting at the end of your fiscal year (marginally), but it has always been my personal preference nonetheless.

When you are deciding on your corporate structure, decide what is best for you based on the advice of your lawyer and your accountant. What you choose as your corporate structure will have implications so make sure you understand each type as clearly as you possibly can.

The easiest and most common form of business structure is the sole proprietorship. A sole proprietorship is a business where the owner represents the company and is legally responsible for it as a person.

Operating a business with a partner appeals to some small-business owners, especially women. The road to entrepreneurship can be overwhelming and it seems like it would be easier and more fun with someone you respect and care about. From my personal experience, partnerships can have enormous benefits in sharing a workload, but if clearly delineated roles are not laid out in the early establishment of the business, along with a partnership agreement, things can become messy very quickly.

I have seen many friendships obliterated by not having a partnership agreement in place. If you are starting a simple business with a partner, you may want to pick up a copy of Self-Counsel Press' *Partnership Agreement* kit. It is inexpensive and effective to create a partnership agreement. I would also recommend consulting a lawyer to make sure you protect your friendship first. The lawyer will be able to guide you through potential scenarios that you may not think of.

As I said earlier, incorporation is the type of business structure I prefer. Although it increases your amount of reporting and usually accounting costs at the end of your fiscal year, it separates your business losses, profits, and expenses from you as an individual.

To register your business, you can go to your local registry office. In the US, you can go to Business.gov, or in Canada, to a Business Development Centre for more information about registering your business.

These days it is easy to register your business by yourself; even to incorporate. There are many useful tools on the Internet, just as long as you use a reliable resource to properly research your decision. To officially file your documents for registration, you only need to go to your local registry office and pay a nominal fee.

2.4 Company history

If your company is not brand new, it is helpful to include a history of its progress to date. This includes how it started and when, the growth over the period of time it has been in business, awards or acknowledgments in the media, strategic partnerships, as well as explanations for variances in revenue growth from year to year.

2.5 Product pricing

Details of your product for your business plan need to include photos, sketches, patterns, and anything necessary for building your products. It also needs to include pricing, your pricing strategy (e.g., why you chose the price), terms of sale, and what your purchase orders will look like. Many new entrepreneurs will be too generous in the pricing of their product — charging too much can obviously limit sales but charging too little can as well.

> "Studies of consumer markets show that discounts of less than 10 percent elicit hardly any customer response. Offers of between 10 percent and 12 percent exhibited a correlation between discount and sales in over half of the cases recorded. Discounts in excess of 13 percent are distinctly linked to increased sales. But the larger the discount, the less likely it is that the brand will maintain its increased share of the market afterward.
>
> Many studies in diverse parts of the world show that high price is associated in the consumer's mind with high quality. This holds especially true where fashion or taste is concerned. Why else would perfumes and champagne sell for such astronomical prices?"
>
> — Andrew Gregson, *Pricing Strategies for Small Business*, (North Vancouver: Self-Counsel Press, 2008).

2.6 Target market analysis

Market research can be a large undertaking. Don't assume going into a business that you will know exactly who your market is. Also don't assume that your market is simple enough to be boiled down into one category (e.g., small-business owners), and never say, "my product is for everyone" because I can guarantee you, you are wrong — and you will be laughed at by potential lenders.

Make sure you understand exactly the kinds of people your ideal clients are. To do this, you can look at your current clients or if you are just getting started, you can use survey tools on the Internet such as SurveyMonkey, which allow you to quickly interview your potential customers and dig deeper into what common characteristics they have.

If, for example, you build a breast-feeding pillow and your current target market is defined as mothers of babies between birth and 16 months old, you may also want to find out what tax bracket they are in, how educated they are, where they live, and what the policies of the public health office in their region advise for breast-feeding. Analyzing your competition and the demographic they serve can provide you with a niche market that your competitors may not be recognizing. For statistics from regional census and government surveys, check out USA.gov or Statistics Canada at www.statcan.gc.ca.

A professional market researcher would use a combination of qualitative and quantitative studies to get the best results. The qualitative component would have essay and open-ended questions while the quantitative would usually be survey-oriented or multiple choice.

Throughout the first couple of years with *The MOMpreneur Magazine*, we used SurveyMonkey frequently. We asked our readers what their favorite components of the magazine were, what kind of marketing opportunities or advertising they would buy, how much they would spend, what their total budget for advertising and marketing was, and how often they referred to the magazine after the month in which it was issued. This allowed us to build our sales plan around their needs for advertising and also allowed us to tailor the magazine's content to suit their needs as entrepreneurs and mothers more closely. The interesting thing we found was that although they loved the entrepreneurial content, the sex, marriage, and shopping articles were also top priority for readers — their work and home lives were often not separated and they wanted the magazine to have the same mix and balance.

2.6a Market share analysis

If you have been in business for a few years, you need to start to consider what your market share is in order to grow your business and take a larger portion of that market share. Here are the steps to figure it out:

1. Define your market before you calculate. Be specific. For example, the sales of Coca-Cola are much smaller than Coca-Cola products, which include all products manufactured by the company.

2. Find out all of the similar products made in your market and the total number of these items.

3. Divide the number of units you have sold by the total number of units sold in the marketplace. This gives you the percentage of your market share.

4. Assess if you are gaining or losing market share. If you are losing, who is taking it and why? If you are gaining it, what are you doing differently?

2.7 Competitor analysis

The term competitive intelligence sounds like something out of a James Bond movie, but in reality it is an essential tool to learning from your competitors. Although I do not advocate focusing on what your competitors are doing or copying them by any means, I do advocate watching their growth patterns, their strategic partners, and their messaging strategies to see what you can learn from. Large companies invest enormous amounts into competitive intelligence, but I think it is the micro business that can learn the most. Compare your business to a larger one with a big budget, see what they are doing, and use that as inspiration to go forward.

Tools that can help you with your competitor analysis can be as simple as setting up a Google Alert so that you are notified every time that company's name appears on a website or in the media. You can also hire a professional firm of data aggregators to monitor and analyze data from public tax returns and financial information. A new free service that makes it even easier is Workstreamer. They watch and give real-time information on competitors, clients, prospects, partners, and vendors.

Information I monitor through social media tools such as Hoot-Suite and Google Alerts include things like what my competitors are saying about themselves, what clients are saying about them, and what niche or needs they are missing. What are their clients needing that they aren't providing, and what can I do to leverage that information?

Use competitive research to —

* find new customers,

* see how economic change affects your market,

* understand how to target your market better,

* forecast for the potential of the market, and

* understand what your competitors are offering.

There were so many women starting new businesses during the conception of *The MOMpreneur Magazine*, but there was not a lot of support for those women. There were networking groups and lending facilities, but there wasn't anyone giving a really honest look at what this lifestyle included. I wanted to provide that information and vehicle for women to form a larger community. I would never have known there was a need for the community without analyzing where women were going for information and support, and how they were building their networks. It was invaluable information.

2.8 Industry analysis

Analyzing your industry is self explanatory. Finding the information you need to see if your business is viable can be a bit more challenging. In the US, go to USA.gov, and in Canada, check out Statistics Canada at www.statcan.gc.ca. For a website with free as well as paid information, go to MarketResearch.com.

Compile statistics that include the following —

ᵈ regions that are experiencing the most growth in your industry,

ᵈ whether or not the market has grown or slowed down and why,

ᵈ what factors have affected its growth, and

ᵈ who the primary players are in the industry.

2.9 Management plan

A management plan is a layout of the human resources needed to fulfill the operations of your business. Which staff will you need to hire to maintain quality and grow the business in a sustainable way? Early on, you will figure out that it can't always be you or a family member you rely on.

If you have anything larger than a microbusiness, you will have to start to grow your team in a fashion that is professional and represents your brand. You will need to consider and include in your management plan the following components before you get into these situations:

ᵈ How will you find these people?

ᵈ How much will they need to be paid?

ᵈ How will they be interviewed, hired, managed, and terminated?

Plan for what your business needs, not what you think you can afford. Once you have put the elbow grease into discovering what your company will really need to thrive, you will probably realize how much more money you need than you originally thought.

Be prepared to continuously update your financial projections while building this plan. If you decide to go to a bank or an investor, this plan and each of its components will be a part of determining your success.

At the beginning of many of my businesses and those in my community, my management team consisted of myself as the CEO, bookkeeper, marketing executive, and janitor — need I go on? If your dream is to create something amazing and influential, you will most likely need to bring in support. Your business plan will help you plan what you will need to do to get to the point where you can hire support.

Whether that is a production manager, operations manager, or just starting with an executive assistant, you need to properly address the person's job description, how much he or she will be paid, what his or her benefits will be, and how he or she will be evaluated. Once you grow your business even further to the point where you have gone to market for outside investors and you have a board of directors, you will have to create a job description for yourself as well. Have sample job descriptions for each integral role in the plan, even if you are months away from hiring each member. See Sample 1 for a job description.

You need to consider how you will evaluate each role. This will not only make you stay on target, but it will give your employees the parameters they need to stay on task and to know what they need to do to be successful and move up within the company. Your evaluation procedure should include items such as —

- how often the evaluations occur,

- the training process that is given to a new employee,

- the key targets that need to be set out for each job description, and

- how the targeted "achievables" in the business plan match up against the actual "achievables" at month end. (This may be difficult to assess in a support position, but qualitative "achievables" that support the budget targets can still be measured.)

Many of the clients I see spend so much time doing the small tasks that can be delegated easily and inexpensively. What you need to focus on as the entrepreneur is the growth of your business, not packaging and shipping the latest $70 order. This is a trap I have fallen into before. I would not properly plan to cover the start-up costs of support labor and would end up doing basic tasks myself. This would ultimately eat up the small amount of time I had while my kids slept. What I should have done and have learned from going forward is that if I only focus my time on sales and growing my business, the business will grow and become self-sufficient — a quality necessary to sell that business down the road.

Something I have recently started doing is partnering with universities and colleges for practicum students needing job placements. Many of these positions are subsidized and these students are eager to please you to get a good grade on their transcripts. They are also looking for a referral or possible job once they have completed their education.

Sample 1
JOB DESCRIPTION

Job Title: Executive Assistant
Salary/Compensation: Depending on experience

1. Department: Administration

2. Reports to: CEO — Kathryn Bechthold

3. Job Objective: To build the systems and procedures of the corporation and to manage customer service for all current accounts.

4. Responsibilities and Accountabilities (principal duties, continuing responsibilities, and accountability):

    a. Managing email and phone inquiries

    b. Managing client database

    c. Managing marketing calendar, alerting CEO to upcoming events, initiatives, etc.

    d. Building a marketing survey to launch for November 2011 with CEO, and collecting data

    e. Billings and basic bookkeeping

    f. Measuring salesperson data

    g. Adding website content twice a week

    h. Compiling newsletter editorial; building the biweekly newsletter

    i. Maintaining sales software

    j. Building relationships with networking and entrepreneurial women's groups across North America

    k. Building and maintaining social media follower list

5. Job Specifications (necessary skills and experience required): Necessary skills include basic computer skills, email marketing capacity, communication skills, networking skills, and online social networking capacity.

6. Salary: $45,000 per year, plus health and dental benefits at $85 per month

7. Evaluation:

    a. Trial period of three months

    b. Evaluations every three months based on negotiated targets

Another option for doing tasks that you should not be spending time on is using a service such as Elance. This is a website that connects people with freelancers from all over the globe. You post your project, you post your budget, and then you wait to have freelancers bid on your project. I have hired virtual assistants to do data entry for $7 an hour in Thailand, a graphic designer in Pakistan for less than $10 an hour, and for the most part, I have had really great experiences. Elance has an escrow service that holds the payment for the completed job until it has been delivered and also allows you to rate the work that was completed. I only hire those freelancers with strong positive ratings who have done a number of jobs similar to the one I am looking to have completed.

2.9a Sales plan

Within your management plan, it would also be helpful to have a separate section for a sales plan. No matter what you are producing, whether it is a service or a product, you will need sales. You cannot rely on those sales to grow organically or by themselves. You will need to market your product as well as follow up with potential buyers. If you have a larger business in mind, you cannot be the only person responsible for sales but you have to be prepared to be the best salesperson on the team and lead them to your objectives.

Depending on your business, you will need to decide on how your sales team will be found, how they will be compensated, and how they will be measured and evaluated. There are so many stories of companies that hire salespeople only to pay them for months and months without seeing a return on their investment, or worse, they see a loss of their investment in that staff member. I also have seen companies offer a position based on 100 percent commission, which causes so much turnover that the companies cannot reach their objectives.

I find the best solution for salespeople is to have a commission-based position with a base salary that increases with performance and grows as new targets are hit and maintained. For example, a new salesperson is hired at 8 percent commission (find your industry standard and also figure out what will need to be sold to make a proper full-time salary) with a base salary of $1,500 per month and a target of $120,000 in sales that should be reached by the end of month three. Depending on what you are selling, this target needs to be reasonable. If you can't achieve it yourself, don't expect a new salesperson to either.

2.10 Strategic alliances

For some businesses, strategic alliances play an important role. At *The MOMpreneur Magazine*, it was an integral part of our marketing plan to partner with business colleges and universities, networking groups, and other networks that had large communities of women in our target market. It allowed us to reach these women in a cost-effective way and benefited the partner by providing free magazines, discounted ads, and sometimes content in the magazine.

When planning for your business, consider what you can offer to potential partners that have large databases of clients in your target market. If you do decide to negotiate an agreement, always put it in writing, get a detailed outline of what each party will provide, and put an end date and a termination option on it. The last thing you need is to be committed to a partner who goes through an ownership change or a change in values that directly influences your credibility.

2.11 Marketing strategies

We will spend more time on your marketing plan in Chapter 8, but this portion of your business plan will be essential to achieving your goals each year. You will need to answer the following questions in this section of your business plan:

- How will you tell your customers about yourself?

- How will you stay on the top of their minds when the time comes when they need your service?

- How will you build word-of-mouth business in your community?

- Most importantly, how much will you budget to achieve these goals?

- What will it cost to advertise on a popular website for your market or in a national magazine? You need to have a strong grasp of what these numbers look like before you plan them into your marketing plan.

2.12 Production processes

Most banks and potential investors will need a detailed outlook on how you plan your production processes. They will assess how you manufacture your product or deliver your services based on a comparison to other processes in the same or similar industries. Be clear on who will provide the service, if it is overseas, how you will pay them in a secure manner, how you will guarantee deadlines, and how it will be evaluated.

To source manufacturers overseas, make sure you investigate thoroughly. Try to use government-based facilities to get referrals and to find out how to know whether a manufacturer is legitimate or not.

In the US, the Census Bureau regularly collects and surveys manufacturers. Use them as a starting point to find manufacturers in your industry. If you go to Manufacturing.gov, you will find information on trade analysis in the USA, government grants, and export services for manufacturers as well as support for entrepreneurs who plan to manufacture in the USA.

In Canada, a consultant at Export Development Canada, (www.edc.ca), can be an important member of your team. He or she can find legitimate vendors and provide some guarantee that you will receive what you paid for in return for your money.

Sourcing raw materials and having prototypes developed can be a slow process. Check out resources such as Mcraesbluebook.com to source raw materials or develop prototypes for your business planning needs.

2.13 Distribution strategies

Strong distribution opportunities are the key to any successful business. If you plan to manufacture a product, don't plan or expect for it to become a success just because it is a great product. For most products, you will need your own or contracted sales teams in different regions, distributors in different countries, and sometimes brokers who will negotiate these agreements for you.

To find professional sales companies, you need to look at each industry individually. For the juvenile and baby product market, there are options out there but not all are created equally. Check out places like www.thegiggleguide.com. To find distributors for other countries, check out Export Development Canada for recommendations or go to other manufacturers' websites to see who represents them in other countries.

To find a broker, you can ask for different distributors' recommendations, but be cautious as this can be a very costly way to move forward.

Once you have an agreement secured, do not rely on it as your sole revenue stream. Look at distribution in other countries and outlets, particularly mass markets, and always continue to sell your product yourself.

2.14 SWOT analysis

A SWOT analysis is a quick way to evaluate your strengths, weaknesses, opportunities, and threats as a company. It can quickly focus you and your team on what needs to be done immediately and what needs more resources allocated to it. Sample 2 is a SWOT analysis from a fictional professional organization firm.

2.15 Operations plan

An operations plan is the basic layout of how your day-to-day operations will be carried out. Decide what the steps are to fulfilling a sale and what positions or contractors are needed to complete them. Also, include what materials will be needed for each piece as well as which external resources or contractors will be needed.

If you are in a business with a lot of technical components that someone outside of your industry will not understand, make sure you define each piece as you go along. This plan is not only for your benefit in growing the company and knowing how you will get there, but for a person who may be interested in buying your company or investing in it as it grows. Don't leave readers of the plan scratching their heads over an acronym that has no meaning outside of your industry.

2.16 Financial plan

If you already own a business, you know that there is never enough money (especially early on). You will always strive for more money and will always need to analyze your spending to see where you can make reductions. If you become efficient at this early on, you will learn how to live lean in tougher times. Even gigantic corporations that look like they roll in money and print it in the basement regularly analyze their spending and reduce. Tough times occur when reductions affect your team, but these reductions are essential to creating sustainable businesses. It is much easier if you do this at the beginning and get your costs as low as possible before moving forward.

While building my business plan for the magazine, I came across a local printer which printed on web printers that could produce an

SWOT ANALYSIS

Strengths	Weaknesses
• Company X provides a service that improves functionality as well as the beauty of the space • A variety of opportunities and pricing is possible • Systematized business that can be franchised for another entrepreneur balancing life with children • Newsletter content is repurposed for website, Twitter, and Facebook	• Expensive endeavor: target market becomes limited due to cost although many in a lower tax bracket need service • All systems for franchising will need to be developed by CEO • No professional support mechanism in place
Opportunities	**Threats**
• Franchising across USA • Growth across North America with website services • Opportunity to develop website consultation • Opportunity to sell and profit from margins on product • Opportunity to profit from commissions from contractors (e.g., carpenter) • Opportunity to build strategic partnerships with realtors, renovation companies, carpenters, contractors • Opportunity to develop expert/celebrity status in writing/speaking • Opportunity for publishing tips, services, etc. • Opportunity to develop following through social media	• Lack of financial capacity to hold market share • Potential for knock-off businesses • Financial capacity to invest in growth and franchising opportunities needs to come from private equity • All growth relies on time and money commitment from CEO. If CEO becomes incapable — business falters

extremely professional looking magazine and had great prices. The printer's only downfall was its minimum order requirement was 5,000 copies more than what I needed and could afford. The salesperson would not budge; he told me it just wasn't worth the company's time to print a magazine on such a small scale.

I called every two days for two weeks brainstorming different options. The salesperson continued to say no and recommended other printers that could serve my needs (at a much higher cost and lower quality). Finally, I baked him a cake. I know it sounds outrageous, but it was a beautiful cake that I worked on all day. I channelled Martha Stewart, called upon Julia Child to possess me, and found it within me and my six-month-old daughter to make an incredible white cake with fresh lemon curd. I even piped little round balls around the top and bottom layers of the cake. I placed that cake in a beautiful box, attached a handwritten note, drove it to the printer's, and left it for the salesperson and the team that worked on that messy, loud web printer day in and day out. The next day, he reduced his minimum for me.

In the weeks to come, he would take me on a tour of the plant and show me every possibility that I could do for a growing magazine, every option he saw other magazines selling to their customers, and he introduced me to the owner of one of the most successful magazine companies in Western Canada.

That relationship was invaluable to a growing company and a newbie, like me, in the magazine business. I was able to call the salesperson and ask about basic terms that I did not understand and if he didn't know the answers, he would find out for me. He gave me referrals to other vendors who I would need in the future, and took me under his wing and showed me what I should avoid and where I could save money but keep the quality look of the product.

The point of this story is to not accept the word "no." Continue to be creative in asking for different options; be persistent until you get the answer and price your business needs.

Your financial plan should include a personal financial summary, start-up costs, your first year cash-flow projection, and a four-year projection.

2.16a Personal financial summary

A list of your personal assets and your personal liabilities should be summarized in your financial plan section. Any bank is going to need to see this summary, and will use it to build a case for you to access credit for your business.

Be careful when taking out credit for your business. I got into trouble signing personal guarantees when the business went under; I was on the hook for those costs. On the flip side, most banks will want some kind of personal guarantee from a new business. If you decide to give one, make sure you hold on to that document and continue to push your bank to remove it as your business grows its own credit rating.

2.16b Start-up costs

The start-up costs section needs to be as detailed as possible and include every piece of information you need to get your business started. Once you have completed the list of items you need, you can return to the list and challenge every cost to see how you can reduce it. You can look for new quotes, ask questions, and remove the go-between in each buying process. You may want to explore overseas labor, manufacturing, or sourcing of raw materials. If you are considering overseas labor, what are the minimum orders for each of these purchases and will others compete with those quotes?

2.16c First year cash-flow projection

The first year cash-flow projection is a summary of your expenses and your incoming revenues in order to cover your expenses and to pay your salary. The cash-flow summary is one of my favorite documents to compile with new entrepreneurs. If they have not done it already, which 90 percent haven't, they get a very real and blunt look at how hard they will need to sell in order to maintain their influx of cash, or how much they will have to continue to invest in order to stay afloat.

Once you have your cash-flow projection completed, you need to look at how long it will take you to become profitable and how much money you will need to cover losses. You will also get your first look at your sales targets for your first year.

You can find the downloadable spreadsheets called Cash-Flow Worksheet and Three-Year Profit Loss Projections on the CD included with this book. Sample 3 shows you a first-year cash-flow projection.

2.16d Four-year cash-flow projections

This section of your financial plan is a "best guess" projection on where you want to be in four years. This is where you get to dream big, but most importantly, learn exactly what you need to sell in order to achieve your dream of a successful company. It is really important for you to dream big in this section. Knowing what you want out of this business and what this business can do for you is essential. This exercise will help you to achieve that dream in a reasonable way — a way that will show prospective lenders or investors that you have planned for this success and that you know how you are going to get there.

3. Review Your Business Plan

Schedule time to review your business plan every six months. By the time you have completed the plan in its entirety, you will have put a tremendous amount of energy into it. Make sure you use it as a living, breathing tool to ensure your success. Plan to make changes, adjustments, and sometimes fresh starts before you get on the right path.

FIRST-YEAR CASH-FLOW PROJECTION

CASH-FLOW PROJECTION	START-UP	JAN	FEB	MAR	APR	MAY	JUN	JUL	AUG	SEP	OCT	NOV	DEC	TOTAL
OPERATING DATA														
Quantity of Product Sold														0
Average Price of Product														0
REVENUE														
Sale of Goods/Services														0
Collection of Accounts														0
Other Revenue Sources														0
Loans/Other Cash Injected														0
TOTAL REVENUE	0	0	0	0	0	0	0	0	0	0	0	0	0	0
COST OF SALES														
Merchandise Cost														0
Receiving Cost														0
Production and Packaging Cost														0
Sales and commission Cost														0
Distribution and Shipping Cost														0
TOTAL COST OF SALES	0	0	0	0	0	0	0	0	0	0	0	0	0	0
EXPENSES														
Salary and Wages														0
Payroll Taxes														0
Professional Services														0
Advertising														0
Travel														0
Insurances														0
Loan Interest														0
Outside Services														0
Postage and Printing														0
Rent/Lease Expense														0
Real Estate Taxes														0
Facility Utilities														0
Repairs/Maintenance														0
Telephone/Fax/Pagers														0
Supplies: Office														0
Software														0
Memberships														0
Subscriptions														0
Training														0
Purchases: Other														0
Capital Purchases: Other														0
Other														0
Sales Taxes														0
Loan Principal Repayment														0
TOTAL EXPENSES	0	0	0	0	0	0	0	0	0	0	0	0	0	0
NET INCOME	0	0	0	0	0	0	0	0	0	0	0	0	0	0
Accumulated Profits/Loss	0	0	0	0	0	0	0	0	0	0	0	0	0	0
LIVING EXPENSES REQUIRED	(Optional)													
Income Taxes														0
Health Insurance														0
Other Needs														0
Income Needed	0	0	0	0	0	0	0	0	0	0	0	0	0	0

YEAR _____

Intellectual Property

"We have paid large amounts of money to protect our intellectual property. It's hard to be totally protected in this industry. It's the nature of the beast. You just have to budget for it."

— Jessica Jacobs, Little Soles Inc.

As your business grows, your intellectual property value does as well. To prevent an enormous investment of time and money being knocked off by someone else with good research skills, make sure you properly protect the developing of intellectual property for your business. This can be done in a variety of ways; to start with, get a non-disclosure agreement completed by anyone you plan to show your business plan to. Self-Counsel Press includes a Secrecy and Non-Disclosure Agreement in its *Employee Management Forms Kit*.

"Being knocked off is just a part of the game; at the same time you have to stay on top of these things. I have called competitors who have done this and confronted them on it. It did make a difference and they have changed their collateral material as a result."

— Anonymous

There are four types of intellectual properties that a businessperson would typically use:

1. Patent

2. Copyright

3. Trade Secret

4. Trademark

Because this delves into subject matter that may need the expertise of a specialized lawyer, I decided to bring one in — and all for the bargain-basement price of this book! Ann Carlsen[1], of Ann Carlsen & Company, provided us the following advice and information about patents, copyright, trade secrets, and trademarks in the following sections **1.** to **4.**

1. Patent

A patent is needed when there is a new invention involved. It involves something usually tangible, so it could be a process or an item such as a cookie, the pen, or the bobby pin. In Canada the parameters are narrow. In some other countries, there are business method patents, but they are not usually applicable in Canada.

If something is patented anywhere in the world, then it cannot be patented in Canada. Many people will travel somewhere, such as Europe, and see an idea they really like and are interested in patenting it; however, it is not patentable by the person who discovers it on their travels. The patent applies only in the country that the patent has been granted.

If someone is interested in patenting her invention, she needs to keep in mind the issue of timing, as a patent must be applied for within one year of the invention being made public. For instance, if you take your invention to a trade show and people are clamoring because this is a great product or idea, you will want to protect your right so that you have the full rights to market and manufacture the invention. You have to do the application within one year of making it public. If you miss that one-year cutoff, then you have a problem. Other people can't patent it (initially) because only the inventor or someone that the inventor assigns the right to can patent it. After that year, if the patent hasn't been filed, then anyone can manufacture and market the idea in Canada and the US. Other countries have shorter patent terms so this

---

[1] Ann Carlsen is also a registered trademark agent for the US. She represents Canadian clients in the US.

is important if you are going to be marketing in other countries. And if you do have an invention, the best thing to do is to go to a patent agent and find out whether it is the sort of thing that can be patented.

A patent can be relatively expensive and could take several years to acquire. You are probably looking at $10,000 – $15,000 and several years per country. If it is something very simple, it could be less than that.

2. Copyright

Copyright is the second thing that people will have as an intellectual property. Copyright is great because it is exactly the opposite of patent, and it doesn't cost anything at all. If you are writing a book, copyright comes into existence and attaches to the writing. The same goes for things such as software, writing, artistic endeavors, and photographs. It's something that is totally creative, and the person who has the copyright is the person who created it, unless it's assigned.

You can register a copyright and there are some advantages for doing so, but it's not a requirement in the US or Canada. In the US, it's more important to register because there are definitely advantages; you are not being able to sue for damages unless you have registered your copyright. Be sure to check with a lawyer to make sure you have covered your bases.

Copyright is international. If you have copyright in the US or Canada, you have that copyright under a copyright convention. It is recognized in most of the countries in the world.

Unless you're adopting something which is really, really old, you should assume there is a copyright to it. That's why everything should be original. I've had clients that thought that their work was original; they've attended courses where they've been provided with what they thought were non-copyright protected designs. When they used these commercially, they would get a cease and desist notice after finding out, to their chagrin, the designs were protected by copyright. Just because you find something on the Internet, does not mean it is public domain.

You don't have to give notice if you have a copyright or necessarily take measures to protect it, but it's always a good idea.

3. Trade Secret

The third property you need to consider is a trade secret. This is something that every business has. Trade secrets are the things that you want to keep secret from your competitors, which are very often business methods. For example, if you are making food, you can use a trade secret to maintain and protect the secrecy of your recipe. However, if you distribute it and make it public, then that confidentiality, the secrecy, is lost forever. The Coca-Cola formula is a trade secret. The company could have patented it, but a patent does not provide protection after it expires, meaning anybody can access it — it's not permanent. It lasts until the inventor or company makes it public.

4. Trademark

The trademark is used to distinguish one person's goods and services from another. It is often taken as the name of the service or the product. Take for example, Kellogg's Corn Flakes; Kellogg is the trademark.

Trademarks are very important because the goodwill of the business is almost always tied up with that trademark. In some cases, if it's one person, sometimes you do recognize the person as the provider of the service or seller of the goods; however, as soon as several people get involved, you recognize the trademark.

Trademarks can be words, numbers, letters, or design elements. Some countries, such as the US, will allow trademarks to include sound and are currently considering scent; Europe also includes gestures. Canadians are very straightforward and do not include scent, sound, or gesture. Make sure to check with your lawyer about what you can trademark in your region.

There are two types of trademarks. There is the common-law trademark, which is a trademark that you haven't registered. As soon as you start using a trademark, it becomes a common-law trademark, which is a trademark that has been used in the marketplace. It doesn't have to be used excessively and the amount of protection that is given by the court to that trademark is extensive for the reputation of that company.

The best kind of trademark is the registered trademark. It is a trademark that has been registered in the state in which you are doing business. As each state in the US has its own rules for trademarking, make sure you budget for some legal guidance on how to plan this into your budget and business plan.

In Canada, only the federal government can allow you to register trademarks. Once you have registered a trademark, you have exclusive rights to use that trademark across Canada. As long as you are using it somewhere in Canada, your trademark is protected throughout the entire country against use, in a more complicated way. A common-law trademark would only protect you in the actual area you have the reputation. If someone was operating in Calgary and another person in Ontario decided to use your common-law trademark, there is nothing you can do about it unless the person in Calgary could show her reputation extended into Ontario. You have to show that the other company was using your reputation to bootstrap itself into the marketplace.

As for when to apply for the trademark, the first step is to go to a trademark agent and to do an availability search as soon as you think you know what your business is going to be called and what your trademark is.

Some people think they have created a very unique trademark and start their business using it without going to a trademark agent. Then two or three years later, once they have got a really great reputation, they receive a letter from a law firm claiming the business is infringing its client's trademark, and to cease or desist immediately, or they will be taken to Federal Court for infringement. You obviously don't want to have to deal with that. While most of those cases can be settled without going to court, the settlement almost always includes the condition the person who received the cease and desist order must stop using that trademark. Now there are two or three years of reputation and goodwill wrapped up in that trademark that the person is going to lose.

It's difficult to change a trademark when a reputation is built up with it. It's costly because you have to inform everybody and do marketing just to let people know that you are no longer ABC or DEF. Therefore, one of the first things to do is an availability search just to make sure that you are not infringing on someone else's trademark. Registering a trademark may cost a couple of hundred dollars, sometimes more depending on the trademark agent, but it is definitely money well spent.

When somebody is starting up, the very first thing she should do is visit the US Patent and Trademark Office or the Canadian Intellectual Property Office. Go to the database and enter the trademark you want and conduct a very preliminary search. If you find somebody who has the same trademark for similar goods and services, or services that you could see yourself providing in perhaps three or four years, or goods and services that people in your business also provide, then move on to your next trademark option.

Although the test for infringement is whether the trademark looks confusingly similar to another, the first thing to determine is if they are exactly the same. If they are exactly the same, move on to another trademark. If you can't find something that is exactly the same, this is the time to go to the trademark agent, because determining your next move when it's confusingly similar is a complex task. You have to look at what they call the "state of the register," which is the number of trademarks that are similar for similar goods and services. The more trademarks there are, the less distinctive the differences have to be.

A trademark agent can help with getting a trademark which is protectable. The process is very similar to Canada: application, review by an examiner, approval, and publication. There are 30 days that anybody can oppose it, and if you are opposed, you have to show you have already used the trademark at the time of filing.

To file your trademark application in the USA, go to the website of the United States Patent and Trademark Office. In Canada, go to the website of the Canadian Intellectual Property Office.

5. Monitoring Your Intellectual Property

Because I trademarked the word "mompreneur" in Canada before anyone else, I was able to ride the success of that word on the heels of the growing trend in North America. No one in Canada could use that word without my permission, and more importantly, the media would not use it without consulting me first. This built my credibility and established me as the "expert" in the field of "mompreneurs." This was a continuing trend until I left the company. This trademark also increased the value of my business when it came time to sell. Not only had the business developed value because of its growth, goodwill, and client base, but because of the trademark it had as well.

I used a trademark lawyer to file my first trademark application. I was very clear on what I wanted to use the word for, but most importantly, I was able to dream very large and write every conceivable idea I could implement under the trademark application. This is important, because if I had only written "a women's business magazine in Canada that incorporates the balance of motherhood," there would have been the risk of being challenged by someone else who wanted to use the word to operate trade shows, a networking group, or something else that I had yet to do or did not have the capital to fund.

From my experience with trademarking the word "mompreneur," it was beneficial, but was a double-edged sword. As much as it grew my profile, it came with an enormous amount of work. As the registered owner of the trademark, it was my job to monitor the marketplace and defend the word if it was being used by an unauthorized user. You can imagine the scope of this job. Today, when I Google the word "mompreneur" I come up with 8,605 links using the word. Obviously not all of these are connected with the original company. Sending a cease and desist to each of these people to protect the trademark, especially to potential clients, became a big job needing someone with finesse to discuss the issue with each user.

Many larger companies can afford to have departments that work only to protect the trademarks of that corporation, but for a mom-owned microbusiness, you will need to do it yourself.

I used a template letter for the cease and desist order and always followed up to make sure the offending company stopped using the word immediately. In the rare cases where someone did not comply, I did not hesitate to bring a lawyer in to protect my rights to the word. If I had left the issue alone, and allowed others to use the word without acknowledging that it was trademarked, I would have been at risk of losing the rights to the word on the corporate level.

4

Building Your Dream Team

One of the tricks to being successful in business is surrounding yourself with people smarter than you. Many entrepreneurs make the mistake of not spending any money, when they begin their businesses, on outside contract services — people that can really make a difference when launching a business from the ground up. The following are the key people you need to have in your business.

1. Childcare Network

You need to have people you can call on for day-to-day childcare or when an emergency arises. Having your children safely cared for on a day-to-day basis or in an emergency is a necessity. There is nothing more distracting then worrying about whether or not your children are being well cared for while you are away trying to build a solid company.

Whether or not you are trying to do this from home while being the primary caregiver, you need to have some backup if a media opportunity comes up, an investor opportunity arises, or you just need 30 minutes to make a phone call without having to stop to change a bum or wipe a nose. This needs to be your first priority — don't leave it until you are desperate.

If you decide to use a traditional day-home or daycare, plan to have a backup caregiver for evening or weekend work. You may need to investigate options for outside of normal business hours or last-minute meetings that you did not have planned.

2. Computer Expert

If you are not already a computer nerd or know one, I suggest you find one — fast. There is nothing more frustrating than staring at a fatally infected computer, which has not been backed up in a long time, or having made a crucial error to your website template when you uploaded, leaving you with a website that looks like it was built by your four-year-old!

Your computer expert should be easily accessible, live in his mother's basement, and be younger than 18 years old — okay, just kidding, but only partially! One of my company websites was hacked and a demonic looking naked woman's image was placed on the homepage — we were notified by a client. Luckily, we have Nic, owner of Nerd Design Group Inc., who was able to quickly respond and have it removed within moments of us discovering it.

3. Banker

It is becoming harder and harder to find a banker that can manage all aspects of your financial needs for you these days, but try to find someone who has immediate access to all of your personal financial information, credit history, and business banking information.

When I owned my charity, our cash flow was more stressful than a financial-planning discussion with my husband. I needed $50,000 every two weeks to meet my payroll but had to wait on government funding to arrive — a risky game of chicken. I cannot tell you how many times my personal relationship with my banker allowed me to call at 8:00 a.m. and have her pull strings to allow us to float until the money came in. This would not be possible had she not had an intimate relationship with our financial situation, a close measurement of my credit management, and a history of payment schedules from our funder. To this day, we are friends that stay in contact, and she has continued to grow her career as well, allowing me more opportunities in her network.

4. Graphic Designer

Many people wrongfully discount the absolute necessity it is to have a professionally designed brand — especially in the early days, when it can make or break a sale. If you look like you have just thrown together your logo, website, and collateral materials, your clients will assume you will do the same with their projects. I read a book by Martha Stewart a few years ago, and one of her keys to success was to "make it beautiful" — no matter what you do, it needs to be beautiful.

5. Virtual Assistant

Most of us dream of having someone on a day-to-day basis to handle the things none of us want to do. Once you are in business, you need to learn to quickly evaluate how much your time is worth. If you know you can close a $5,000 sale in one hour, you should not be spending any time packaging and shipping, something you can delegate for a handful of dollars an hour. All of your time should be focused on closing sales, driving traffic to your business, and building your market share.

6. Vendors

As you get further and further into a business, you begin to rely on key vendors that make your business successful. Learn who has your back and who doesn't. Regularly compare pricing and ask for competitive deals. When you have found people willing to go the extra mile for you, make sure you do the same for them. Does it really help them if you pay in 15 days instead of 30? Or does it make them really excited when you send referrals their way? Make sure you find out what makes your vendors tick and regularly work on building those relationships.

7. Media Connections

Once you build your media connections, whether they are relationships with popular bloggers, news anchors, or freelance writers, you can never let them falter. Compliment them on other stories (that were not about you) so you remain on the top of their minds. Send your media connections Christmas cards or story leads — and always thank them after they interview you.

8. Your Community

As you build your network of clients, colleagues, vendors, and media contacts, make sure you continue to stay in touch. Whether that is inviting them to an anniversary party every year, regularly commenting on their tweets and Facebook activities, supporting their charities, or just sending a quick note to say hi, maintain those relationships as a marketing objective.

9. Bookkeeper and Accountant

Keeping your accounting books constantly current is a lesson that has taken me a number of frustrating experiences to learn. Whether you need to calculate how much you have invested so far to see what you need to sell in the next few days, or need to report to your investors, you need these documents on hand. You need to be in control of your money so that you can make intelligent choices on a quick and timely basis. You will also save a tremendous amount of money if you don't need someone to dig through a year's worth of receipts to figure out what you have been doing financially.

10. Commercial Lease Agent

If you are going to rent or own commercial space, you need to have a professional that you can trust, and who will walk you through the ins and outs of this process. Part of the reason I got into trouble on my first business was that I had signed a personal guarantee on a five-year lease. The business tanked after two years in the space. That left me with no business, a contract that I thought I understood, and a landlord who would not let me sublet. Today, I know in most areas (and especially in this economy), you can negotiate out of a personal guarantee and make a more flexible agreement in case things don't go as planned.

11. Lawyers

There are lawyers who specialize in business, litigation, intellectual property, trademark, and patents to name a few areas. Knowing how much lawyers cost per hour is intimidating especially when you need one in a hurry. Make sure you ask those around you for referrals for good lawyers, and understand what each kind of lawyer does and why you might need one.

Never take a solicitor's word for it that he or she can handle a small litigation. Check the lawyer's references and consider the person's personality. Every so often you need a collaborative lawyer, but sometimes you just need a bulldog. You don't want to get stuck in a tense situation with the wrong lawyer. Also, never represent yourself, especially in the early days of being an entrepreneur. Make sure you get good advice early on before you are faced with a litigious situation.

Esther S. Chung, of Chung Law Corporation, gives the following advice:

"If you want to go for more specialized advice, consider a firm that can handle your areas between all of its lawyers. Then, your contract lawyer can have the firm's family lawyer review the spousal clause for a fraction of the cost than if a different family lawyer had to go through the initial consultation with you again. Or find a lawyer who is able to refer you to other specialists that he or she has worked with before for the parts that he or she cannot handle. No lawyer likes to work with bad lawyers, so it is a good sign.

And as business lawyers do not usually provide free consultations, what often happens is a person sees a lawyer for an initial consultation, and just goes with them (as long as nothing seems wrong). If you are not certain that you do want to go with the first lawyer, then it may be a good investment to pay for a second consultation with another lawyer. A few hundred dollars up front may save you thousands of dollars later.

If you ever need litigation help (someone is suing or you need to sue), you must be sure to pick the right lawyer. Litigation is one area where the cost is indeterminable, and can vary in the tens of thousands of dollars. If you want to try and settle, but your lawyer is out for blood, or you want the lawyer to fight harder, but the lawyer keeps trying to make you take a bad settlement (in your opinion), then you may not be getting efficient representation. The right lawyer requires the requisite level of experience (is it a tough case?), but also needs to be on the same page as you.

How your lawyer behaves can also affect the behavior of the opposing party. (Do you need a tough lawyer to stand up to a bully? Or will the other party only dig their heels in if your lawyer pushes too much weight around?) Again, there are no hard and fast rules. Just gauge how your lawyer reacts to your problem, what the lawyer has to say, and if you ever think the lawyer isn't quite getting you, you may need to see someone else. Again, a few hundred dollars up front can save you tens of thousands later."

11.1 Finding a lawyer to help you set up your business

Finding a lawyer to help make some of these initial decisions may be costly but worth it in the long run. When you start planning for the conception of a business, you may need to look at hiring different lawyers for advice to get you started the right way.

Many lawyers who deal with small business will be able to handle the majority of these issues for you. Just make sure that you have someone who is able to advise you from experience on each of these potential situations:

- **Business law:** To discuss corporate structure and negotiate partnership agreements.

- **Securities law:** If you plan for your business to go public in order to fund its growth.

- **Real estate law:** If you plan on purchasing space in order to run your business or you plan to negotiate a leasing agreement to rent space. (This was an area I got into trouble with once by signing a personal guarantee. When that business went under, I was personally responsible for the remaining amount on the lease agreement, which ultimately turned into a very costly mistake.)

- **Employment law:** If you plan to take on employees.

- **Intellectual property:** If you plan to trademark, develop patentable ideas, or publish information.

- **Tax law:** If a significant amount of money is invested.

- **Family law:** If you and other shareholders want to protect business property from family claims, or if you want to be prepared for a potential marriage breakdown.

Hiring and Managing Your Team

"When I make more money, my staff makes more money."

— Erica Ehm, YummyMummyClub.ca

Every entrepreneur with a dream of something bigger comes to the point where they realize they cannot continue to do everything themselves. They quickly review their options, consider their cash flow, and often dive into hiring staff without considering all of the work that goes with management of a team, even if the team is only one person.

As most businesses grow, many entrepreneurial women quickly become burnt out with all of the day-to-day operations, sales, invoicing, and raising of a family. It only takes one child with the stomach flu and a few days of sleep deprivation before you realize that you cannot keep your business growing in a sustainable fashion if the entire company is on your shoulders. It also becomes clear that it is in your best interest to do what you do best and to delegate the rest, especially if the rest includes jobs that can be delegated for a relatively low cost.

1. Finding Good Employees

In today's economy, it is often not difficult to find staff to come on board. The difficulty is keeping them happy and growing in their positions for a long period of time. Finding a great employee is a bit like winning the lottery. It is not easy finding great people who are committed to your dream, and when you do, you want to do everything you can to maintain the positivity of that relationship. Replacing a full-time employee can be a costly and stressful experience, especially if the person leaves on sour terms.

Hiring a bad employee is a bit like having the stomach flu, except it doesn't go away with a bit of Imodium. Instead, it continues until you reach your breaking point and fire him or her after days or weeks of low productivity, lost time on training and evaluation, and the stress of the termination.

Questions to ask yourself include:

♥ Do I really need this person?

♥ Do I understand the ins and outs of the job description, and have I tried to do it myself?

Without knowing the position you will not know how much it is worth to you, how much time it takes, how to train someone else to do it, and, most importantly, how to evaluate the skills of a potential employee in that position.

Finding the right people becomes one of your most challenging tasks as your business grows. What I have learned over the years is to constantly look for people I want to work with. I collect names, business cards, and résumés, and I keep them on file (with their permission) until I have a need for them. If I can't use them, I try to pass their names along to a colleague who is looking for someone to fill his or her employee needs. The benefit of this is that when it does come time to hire, I already have a database of individuals and connections that can lead me in the right direction. Do not wait until you lose a staff person the night before a big event, vacation, or sales opportunity.

When you do have to go to a service to find people to hire, you need to consider your options. Something like Kijiji.com or Craigslist.org, while economical, will only elicit an enormous amount of résumés that may or may not fit your job description. This will not only waste your time but will be an exercise in frustration. Using an advertising tool such as Monster.com or Workopolis.com, while an investment financially, will help you find the right candidate by allowing you to hone the requirements of the position and describe your corporate culture. If you have a smaller budget, consider using social media to describe the ideal candidate to your network and communities. I have found quite a few treasured employees just by asking for referrals. It was inexpensive, quick, and they were great employees.

The biggest thing to remember is that great people want to be involved in projects that challenge them, matter to them, and that they have a vested interest in. I have purposely kept my businesses small because of the fact that I like to work from home while my children are young and I believe it builds a focused team that knows the financial limits of the company, and the quality necessary on the output of the projects or products. It is also financially sound; I spend little to no money on overhead, leaving me with a much stronger profit at the end of every month.

I have learned to ignore résumés. They are often exaggerations of the truth and reduce experiences to a few lines under each past position. I do look at cover letters. I search for writing skills, because so much of business is conducted via email. I also look for like-minded values and interests, and I search for someone who has made an effort to challenge himself or herself by pursuing more challenging positions and growing with a company.

2. Interviewing Potential Employees

Before I ever get to an interview, I have a job description in place that is forward thinking. I know where my business is going over the course of the next five years and I know where this position will fit. This gives me the ability to interview someone with questions that suit the position now, but it also allows me to look toward the future to see how he or she will fit in the long run.

In my first company, we hired a tremendous amount of entry-level staff to work with children with neurological disabilities. Because our clientele was disabled, sometimes aggressive, and demanded physical strength on a day-to-day basis, our turnover was high. That, combined with a low salary because of government funding regulations, meant our staff usually didn't last past one year. Because of this, I and my manager became very adept at recognizing quality people in the interview. As women, this is where that gut feeling we're known for really came into play.

Before interviewing, spend some time getting to know what you can and cannot ask; note that an inadvertent question or comment in a conversation can get you into trouble. Here are some topics to stay away from:

- Race or color; questions about complexion, coloring, color of skin

- Religion or creed

- National origin, ancestry, native tongue

- Gender

- Marital status

- Children or birth control, or any question around family planning — you also cannot ask the ages of an applicant's children

- Birthplace, birth date, or age

- Photograph — an applicant cannot be asked to attach a photograph for an interview or at any time before hiring

- Citizenship — you can ask, "Are you a citizen, or if not, do you plan to become one?" However, you cannot ask if the applicant is naturalized or native born or to produce citizenship papers. You cannot ask which country the applicant is a citizen of.

- Arrest record — although you can ask, "Have you ever been convicted of a crime?" and then ask for details. You cannot ask, "Were you ever arrested?"

- Address or duration of residence

- Disability; however, you can ask if they have any impairment that would impede them from applying for the position for which they have applied, but not if they have a disability in general

Key features to look for in interviewees:

- I look for people who have researched the position and the company that holds it. If they haven't been to the company website or Googled the company, the interview is terminated without any further time invested.

- I look for people who ask a lot of questions about how we do things and why. Asking questions shows an interest in the position as well as an interest in a higher-level position rather than someone who is just told what to do.

❦ I look for someone who will represent me and my brand in a professional manner. If the person has done his or her research and has looked at any of my company's websites, the person will know that lip rings and blue hair do not fit my brand. That being said, I do look for people who are creative, think outside the box, and challenge the status quo to make things better.

❦ I look for someone who has done his or her research on a competitive salary in the industry of the business, and who is strong enough to defend his or her position for the salary he or she is requesting.

❦ I ask a lot of experiential and behavioral questions. Asking, "Do you work well under pressure?" will elicit a simple "yes." Instead, I ask about a stressful situation that the person was in where he or she had to complete a project on deadline and how he or she was able to do so. This will give you a better sense of the candidate's skill set because he or she has to describe the situation and how he or she reacted under pressure.

Other questions I like to ask include:

❦ Have you ever disagreed with a coworker in the past and were you able to resolve the disagreement?

❦ Have you ever suggested a new revenue stream for a business?

❦ What do you see as the target market of my business? How would you approach the target market?

❦ Have you ever performed poorly and had to reorient how you completed your work in order to be successful?

❦ What makes you think you are better qualified for this position than other candidates?

Another concept to consider is your corporate culture. In all of my businesses, one key component is having fun. I do not enjoy working with people who consider every challenge a crisis, or who complain about tiredness, busyness, or me. I prefer employees who have issues, to find a solution and bring it to me to discuss. I don't want to work with people who are not creative in their thinking and strong in their ability to find a solution to a situation that is uncomfortable.

3. References

I have never hired someone without checking his or her references first. I do look for whether the reference was a supervisor or not (I only accept management as a reference) and how long ago they worked together. I recently checked a reference for someone and the reference didn't remember the person. The reference had to look up the person in the database to make sure that the person had worked there before. If the person worked there and used someone who could not remember him or her, it was a big red flag that the person had not had a positive employment experience. I want to hire someone that is really going to "show up" for the position, be self-motivated, and show me how he or she can improve my business; otherwise, it is just a big waste of my time.

I always ask the reference the following questions:

- Did this employee complete tasks in a timely manner and did he or she meet your expectations?

- Did the person get along well with other team members? Were there ever any conflicts?

- Did you ever give the person constructive criticism? For what? How did he or she handle it?

- Would you hire this person again?

Once you have found the right employee, you need to lay out the position with a job offer. The offer needs to include the position, the location in which the work will be done, the payment, the expenses that will be reimbursed, the benefits, and how the position will be evaluated after a trial period.

Hiring and managing staff is a big job with a tremendous amount of legal ramifications. Make sure you understand the legal requirements for employment in your area and follow them. Also, make sure that if the person is not working out, you have the flexibility to terminate him or her quickly and cost effectively.

On the CD you will find an Offer of Employment Letter for you to use in your business.

4. Evaluations

Evaluations are never an easy task to complete but essential to the growth of an employee. The evaluations limit risk to the corporation — if you have been having issues with an employee that have required constructive feedback and then a written warning, it is important to note these in the review. If you are forced to terminate in the future, having this documentation is essential — especially if there is any question of wrongful dismissal. Evaluations also give you an opportunity to say thank you to your employee.

I find many women have difficulty giving feedback when it is a criticism of work completed, especially when it is someone that they care about and work with closely. Often, these things are left unsaid until there is a breakdown in the relationship and each party vents their frustrations all at once, overwhelming the discussion and damaging the relationship. If the expectation of a performance evaluation is established at the time of hiring, then it will be expected on the time line laid out. This eliminates the need to surprise your employees with the scheduling of the meeting and it also allows them to see it as a professional growth opportunity, not an opportunity for them to be embarrassed.

During an evaluation, I like to ask the following questions:

- **Can you describe your job description to me?** This allows me to understand what they think their role is in comparison with my idea. If I am frustrated with their focus on current clients and not looking to acquisitions, this will give me a clear indication of the miscommunication.

- **Do you have the support you need to do your job? Is there anything missing?** As an entrepreneur and a mom, I am often so busy, I sometimes do not recognize when a staff member is needing more one-on-one time with me either for training, support, or to work out an issue. This gives the person an opportunity to discuss the situation. Sometimes the answer is as simple as, "I really need to change my schedule to allow for a school volunteer position once a month," or "I need to be able to meet with you at least once per week to help complete this project." If you have hired a thoughtful employee who is strong enough to communicate his or her needs in order to achieve his or her objectives, then this will usually be an easy fix.

- **Have you received the training you need in order to move forward?** Often, one of the biggest mistakes an entrepreneur makes is being too busy to properly train and support the team member she hires in the first few months of the position. This is a great way to find out if you have been guilty of this and whether or not you can resolve it quickly may mean the difference between employee retention or loss.

- **Do you understand the five-year plans of the company?** If your employee does not understand your targets, he or she will not be able to fully engage in achieving those goals, nor will the person feel like he or she is an integral part of the team.

- 🛒 **What are your five-year plans? Are you looking for something more challenging, higher pay, or a work-from-home option?**

On the CD you will find an Employee Evaluation template for your use.

5. Motivating Employees

"If I was leaving early for the afternoon on a Friday and I knew we had achieved what was needed to be done for the week, I would call my assistant and tell her to go home. I knew she had three boys at home and didn't get a lot of down time. Allowing her an afternoon by herself at home every month or so made a big difference to her."

— Catherine, Des Moines, Iowa

Sometimes motivating staff through pay increases is difficult, especially in a small or new business. Every manager needs to become comfortable with ways to motivate that stand outside of the normal pay increase or pat on the back. Here are some ideas for small business managers:

- 🛒 **Time off:** Sometimes it's as simple as time off.

- 🛒 **Recognition and attention for a job well done:** Everyone likes positive feedback, so make sure you give it constructively and often.

- 🛒 **Flexibility in work area:** For some positions in my office, I don't care when or where the work is done, just as long as the achievables are met. This is a huge bonus for a working mom or someone with a complicated schedule.

- 🛒 **One-on-one coaching for career development:** If you see an employee really excelling in his or her position, train the person to take on more responsibility. Not only does this increase the employee's job satisfaction but it also allows you more time to focus on growing your business.

- 🛒 **Job titles:** Everyone likes a great title. If you can't afford to give a pay raise, consider changing the title of the person to something that the employee will feel proud of. Although it does not sound like much, a person's job title has a lot to do with his or her self-esteem, self-worth, and job morale. Make sure the employee is happy with it.

🛒 **Social gatherings:** I know how busy you are, and if you have a moment of spare time, it usually goes to something like sleep or getting groceries, but scheduling time with your staff outside of the office can make an enormous difference to your working relationship.

🛒 **Casual dress day:** As a working mom, there have been moments when wearing my sweats to my office is a perk of being an entrepreneur. Let your staff enjoy it occasionally as well, as long as you set boundaries (e.g., not in front of clients).

🛒 **Having a laugh:** As I put more years into owning my own business, I realize that it will always be intense and often stressful; having people work with you who make you laugh can be an enormous opportunity to increase job satisfaction. If you have an opportunity, try to include gags and jokes into your company's culture.

🛒 **Autonomy:** If I am looking for employees that will work independently and be self-motivated, I like to encourage them to be a part of making their job satisfaction great. I ask what projects they would like to be a part of, which ones they would like to lead, and what we can do better at as a company. If they have a great idea, I let them make it happen.

🛒 **Flexibility:** Try offering flexible opportunities with childcare. As a mom with young children myself, I brought my baby to work with me every day for a year. When I hired my assistant, she also had a baby younger than one year old. I made it clear that if my baby was allowed, so was hers. Of course, I made it clear when the babies needed to be elsewhere when a client came in, but for the most part, we were able to make it work. The babies were happier as well. Interestingly, we found that many of our clients began to bring their children to the meetings. It just became a part of our corporate culture.

🛒 **Money:** Compensate your staff fairly, give performance-based evaluations, and act on them.

6. Using Virtual Staff

As most entrepreneurial women start their businesses from home, learning to manage a virtual staff is a skill that you will definitely need to acquire. As businesses grow, women often bring outside staff into their homes in order to make key employees accountable or just to improve communication. This becomes complicated, especially when you are trying to separate your personal life from your business. To this day, I dislike team members lifting up my kids or establishing a closer relationship with them. It feels too personal and uncomfortable because a boundary is being crossed. I became quite clear about communicating those boundaries once I decided I preferred working from home, but it took some practice.

For me, I have enjoyed the opportunity to build positions that work virtually. This allows me to hire the best people, no matter where they live, as well as to establish jobs that allow women to work while being the primary caregiver to their children, a value about which I am passionate.

In order to make this work, I have found that I need to do the following three things:

- Hire employees I trust that work well independently.

- Foster communication and personal relationships through creative means including using software such as an Instant Messenger tool. It is really difficult to be available to everybody all the time, especially as an entrepreneurial mother, but being available to your staff can be the difference between keeping them long term or not.

- To establish targets and measure their completion at the end of every week.

With my BlackBerry or laptop, this allows me to be at the doctor's office with my child, watching soccer practice, or making supper, and still be able to quickly give direction in order to maintain productivity.

Finding virtual staff is becoming easier these days. Attend a women's networking group and you are almost sure to find a virtual assistant, and if that doesn't work, just Google one in your area. The benefit of using a contractor such as a virtual assistant is that the person is not your employee, so you are not responsible for the taxes and filing that goes along with having employed staff.

If you are only looking for a temporary position such as someone for data entry or bookkeeping, consider using someone in a different location. Post a job opportunity to a place like Elance.com and have people from all over the world bid on the position. As entrepreneurial women, we are redefining how we make a business and a family work. Do not feel compelled to follow the traditional models of a business, including employment structures, in order to make your company work.

7. When Trouble Arises

It is usually easy to see a disgruntled employee emerge in an organization; it is how you deal with the person that can be challenging. When workplace performance slips, a small business has no choice but to address the problem immediately. You cannot afford to be afraid of offending the person, or worried she will leave because you have called her out on something that should have been done differently. If push came to shove and you had to defend a termination in court, you want to make sure you had the documentation that says you notified the employee, how you tried to remedy the situation, and the date on which it occurred.

A written warning usually follows a verbal discussion but clearly outlines that the conversation was not enough to make it known to the employee that he or she is not performing to the standards of the corporation. If you see that the employee is not working out and the probationary period has past, you want to be able to show that you acted in a way that was fair to the employee. A typical follow up to inappropriate conduct would be a verbal warning, a written warning, a final warning, and then termination. Failure to do so in certain regions could result in a complicated wrongful termination lawsuit.

> "A couple of years into my business, I had a project manager lose his temper in front of a client. While it was pretty intense for a couple of minutes, I managed to end the meeting gracefully and respectfully; a miracle given how young and inexperienced I was at the time. I then took the contractor to lunch to remind him what I expected of him both behaviorally and within the confines of our contract and how we both could have handled the situation differently to avoid a repeat scenario. Difficult? Yes. Necessary? Absolutely.

Whether it's a contractor who isn't listening or staff members who aren't getting along, it's crucial to take responsibility for how situations are unfolding and to be accountable for the outcome. The success of your business depends on it."

— Erica Swanson, Erica Swanson Design

On the CD you will find a Progressive Disciplinary Warning form.

8. Termination

"My experience terminating my employee did not go so well. I began by telling my assistant that I needed someone I could rely on and that lately her lateness, frequent days off, and missing of deadlines was negatively affecting my business — that I had to let her go. She began to cry, really cry. I felt so bad, I started to cry as well. I got it done, but it was a bit messy."

— Karla, Whitefish, Montana

When push comes to shove, no one likes to have to fire someone, especially someone that you have invested time and money into. As mothers and nurturers, terminating a bad apple, or worse, a good apple in a bad economy, is enough to send the toughest entrepreneurial woman to the kitchen for beer and ice cream!

Termination is difficult, not only for the manager or owner, but for your bottom line. Conservative estimates put the cost of terminating an employee beginning at $10,000 for the expense of severance, interviewing and hiring a new employee, and training that person so that he or she succeeds where the last one failed. Those estimates can quickly grow into the cost of that employee for one year, just to replace him or her. Once you have been through this a few times, I guarantee you will learn to look closely at who you hire, evaluate their references aggressively, and train new employees as much as you possibly can.

If the deed must be done, I believe women can use their skills as nurturers to make the best of an awful situation. Here are a few tips:

- ♥ Choose a time of day when few people are in the office to prevent as much embarrassment for the employee as possible.

- ❦ Invite a third person to protect yourself from wrongful termination suits, as well as any possible verbal abuse that may come your way. Sometimes a neutral third party can keep angry words at bay.

- ❦ Keep it short and sweet. Ideally you have already given the person warning so this should be no surprise. Make sure you clearly communicate the termination, and why and what will happen next, even if that is his or her final paycheck and a handshake.

- ❦ Consider consulting a lawyer if the staff person was in your company for longer than three months and the events surrounding his or her termination are unclear, or you feel the employee may take legal action.

- ❦ Be professional and wish the person good luck in his or her future endeavors.

Go home and relax, there is nothing more stressful as dealing with a difficult employee. If the termination has been completed and the employee's dignity was preserved, you have done a good job.

The CD includes a Termination Letter and Termination Checklist for your use.

6

Research

The more years I spend as an entrepreneur, the more I realize you need to become a generalist at everything, just the same as with our children. The first time we hold a baby in our arms, most of us are scared out of our wits with the thought of caring for such a tiny, delicate being. By baby number two, you give birth and are ready and prepared for this next adventure, and by baby number three, you juggle them in the air when they get fussy. The same goes for business: Year one, you are terrified at the thought of upsetting a client by standing up for yourself, you hire everything out because you don't believe you can do it yourself, and the idea of something going terribly wrong is enough to turn your bowels to ice water.

Unfortunately, things do go wrong, manufacturers miss deadlines, shipments don't arrive, employees betray your trust, and every so often, on the morning that payroll is due, you are ready to beg, borrow, or steal to make it through. These are the dirty little secrets of being an entrepreneur that no one talks about, but we all experience. The more comfortable you get with your ability to handle these situations on your own, the more confident you will be in growing your business safely and strategically.

Luckily, you can learn to do anything you want if you know how to use the Internet. On a regular basis, I use the Internet to fix problems around my office. When my computer went on the fritz, I was able to type in the error codes and fix it myself. When I wanted to add podcasts to my community relations campaign, I Googled how to do it. When I began to hire staff, I became very friendly with the sites that support employers' understanding of labor laws in my region. When my company grew to the size where we needed investment dollars from a professional investment firm, I went into that negotiation having done my research, so that I could make my time with the lawyers as short as possible and use them effectively and efficiently.

From my research, I also learned that more than 80 percent of entrepreneurs that take on outside investment are no longer the CEOs of their companies within 24 months. This tidbit of information was the key to me being able to protect myself on an ongoing basis throughout that period of time when I used private equity. Although things were good when it started, as time moved on and a recession hit, I carefully continued to collect pertinent information just in case things went south. Going into negotiations for the termination of that agreement, I had emails from them saying what a great job I had done, I had all of the board meeting notes and approved minutes digitally and in audio format (with members' permission), and I had researched a lawyer who specialized in this kind of work.

The bottom line is to trust that you can handle whatever challenge comes your way if you know how to research the information for you to move forward. Learn how to research effectively and use it to your advantage.

Resources you should look at: Google (my best friend); law schools close to your area, as many will give advice free of charge for the learning experience (the only downfall is that it sometimes takes a few weeks for them to get back to you); the government: I have been in a few situations that could have cost me if I didn't understand the government's needs properly, but each time I called the department I was involved with for help, and they were more than happy to participate. University libraries are also a key research tool for anything you can't find on the Internet. Most librarians will help you answer a question you can't figure out on your own. Lastly, you need to go out and network, and have the guts to ask anyone you think might have a clue about your question. Most experienced entrepreneurs will have been there before and will be able to guide you in the right direction — these are not the times to be hiding your cards. If you need help and you can't pay to hire someone, ask for it.

1. Sourcing Raw Materials

You need to consider looking overseas to source out your manufacturing or raw materials. In this day and age, unfortunately for our countries and for the environment, it is often less expensive to buy product from Asia and ship it west than it is to purchase it here in North America. Buyer beware on this one, as although you will save money, there are just as many horror stories of product arriving mislabelled, produced poorly, or damaged, with no recourse to get your money back. In order to protect yourself against this risk, always ask for North American references, samples, and ideally go and visit the plants to make sure it is a company that is real and following practices you believe in. I may be dating myself, but I distinctly remember the fiasco Kathie Lee Gifford had in manufacturing her women's clothing line. She put her name on a product that ended up being manufactured by child laborers — definitely not a typical value of an entrepreneurial mom.

Some of the greatest amounts of your time will be eaten up researching the right sources for your raw materials, packaging, shipping, and building relationships with the providers. I see so many entrepreneurs stop at the first or second company they call because they don't believe they will find anything better.

Make sure you look at every provider possible because saving 5 percent on a few different items could mean the difference between a tight cash flow and one that pours in. You must know your numbers, such as what all of your raw materials cost, what your cost of time is, what the cost of the space you are using (even if it is your home) is, and what your administration costs are. You need to focus on getting the best price available. Sometimes, the best price may not be the cheapest, but it will give you the best return on your investment. Just make sure you have done the research to know that you have made the correct connection.

2. Sourcing Manufacturers

When it comes time to find the right manufacturing company for your business, you may need to consider looking overseas to get the right price for your bottom line. This can be intimidating; you need to consider cultural differences, communication breakdowns, and miscommunications about details essential to getting your product done right.

If you are able to keep it within the country you live, and are able to make the profit margins needed to sustain yourself, congratulations — it is not an easy feat! If it is something you are intent on doing, look at social enterprise initiatives such as trade schools needing teaching opportunities or even skilled community groups looking for work. A good friend of mine decided to manufacture a knitted children's apparel line. In order to keep the manufacturing in Canada, she went to the Immigrant Women's Association in her area and hired a group of women that had just come over as refugees to knit the apparel line. She was able to pay them a reasonable wage that met the labor laws, and the women were overjoyed with having the work. She maintained her quality and look of the hand-knit product, and the ladies were able to start working immediately, often without needing to find outside childcare options. It was a win-win situation that also transformed into a publicity opportunity in the media because it was so unique.

To find overseas manufacturers and to get initial quotes, check out sites such as GlobalSources.com or Alibaba.com. A North American resource would be MacraesBlueBook.com.

Once you have decided to go forward with ordering, make sure you use a government service for support in ensuring it is a reputable company, getting references, and getting a guarantee that when you pay them, you will get something in return.

3. Reducing Costs on Every Level

As an entrepreneur, because you become so busy in your day-to-day operations, it is sometimes difficult to stand back and get a good picture of your business from an objective point of view. Many women I meet continue to overspend because they have not spent the time working out their budget, asking their team to understand the budget, and then making sure everyone sticks to it. A budget can become a complex thing when you take a close look at every item. It is not just manufacturing and shipping costs you need to look at, but things such as your office supplies count as well.

I remember hiring a fabulous assistant years ago that did everything so quickly and efficiently, it made my head spin. I saved buckets of money in labor costs because, although I paid a bit more per hour for her, she had everything done with less handholding from me since she had the experience and education to make sure it was done correctly. I was saving money on her position, but where I began to lose money was the fact that I had not limited her budget on purchases to get these things done. I assumed she would choose the least costly items when having to make purchases mainly because I spoke about our budget regularly; in reality, she chose the items that worked well and could be delivered in a timely fashion, which meant they were more expensive. Where we broke down was the fact that I had not included her in the development of the budget and I had not given her the duty of getting those purchases made by doing the research first, submitting a proposal for the budget, and then having her move forward.

In the end, it was my fault for not including her in our cost-saving initiatives. From that point on, she became a real leader for the team on taking cost-saving initiatives. She would research sales, make purchases from businesses that were closing, and remind everyone to turn the lights out at night and reuse recycled paper for notes. She was fantastic. Unfortunately, she moved away a few years later to be closer with her children, but because of her, I learned to evaluate my costs on a monthly basis. It is also one of the first things I do when evaluating the functionality of the businesses with which I am consulting.

4. Learning to Automate Your Business

Unless you are one of the select few that thrive on everything being technical and done on computers, you are like me and are learning at a continuous rate — although slower than the 12-year-old next door — how to make technology work for your business.

Learning to automate your business for revenue streams that take little to no energy is ideal for the entrepreneurial mom. If you can come up with something that someone pays for online and then is delivered without you even knowing until that payment falls into your account, you are on the road to real success.

There have been some great businesses out there that have really mastered this skill. A model such as iStockphoto.com is a perfect example. Graphic designers and people in marketing and media fields use this site to download stock images, audio, and videos. They enter their account, search for the right piece of stock, go to the checkout, and pay. Within moments, their computer is downloading content and the person that built that site has put little effort into making that transaction go through. New content is constantly uploaded by users as well. In the end, the owner really just has to focus on the marketing of the business in order to survive.

Even something as simple as adding a sign-up button to an online newsletter is automating the process of connecting regularly with your clientele. It is a simple addition of coding to your site, and then interested parties can sign up for your newsletters without you having to take their information and add it to an email marketing software system.

The companies I like are MyMailout.com, ConstantContact.com, and AWeber.com.

Another system I love is an automated payroll service. Services like these are as simple as entering in the pertinent information of your staff every two weeks, the time sheets are entered, and paychecks complete with pay stubs are sent through direct deposit and email and your tax deductions are submitted, which is a brilliant system for the overworked entrepreneur. Even records of employment are handled, and at the end of the year, your payroll is perfect. Services I prefer are ADP at www.adp.com (or www.adp.ca in Canada) and Ceridian at www.ceridian.com. Both are available in several countries.

Case Study: Baby Gourmet Foods Inc.

Baby Gourmet Foods Inc. launched in 2005 at a local farmers' market in Calgary, Alberta, Canada. It quickly became the go-to place for new moms who wanted wholesome, tasty, and organic baby foods for their growing children. As the demand began to far exceed the resources to maintain the business, CEO and Founder, Jennifer Broe, and her sister, Jill Vos, decided to stop operations and rebuild their business plan with North American distribution as a target.

The following is an interview I conducted with Jennifer Broe.

What made you start Baby Gourmet Foods?

I have always had an appreciation for good food and a passion for cooking, so when my daughter was six months old I dedicated my time to creating her interesting and flavorful meals. Other moms quickly noticed my baby was eating better than their entire family and asked if they could pay me to make some for them. At that moment I realized there had to be a huge market of women longing for a quality, tasty baby food in the market. After some research, I found there had been no innovation in the industry and baby food on the shelves had been overprocessed, tasteless, and, in short, pretty disgusting. I asked the question, "Why would anyone feed their baby something they would never eat themselves?" I wanted moms to feel good about what they were feeding the most important member of the household and from there Baby Gourmet was born.

How important was it to you to get the best, most wholesome ingredients?

Besides food safety, our ingredients and taste profile are one of the most important aspects to our company. When I purchase food for my family, I take the time to source the best products and ingredients, so it was natural for me to do the same for my customers. We start with 100 percent organic ingredients and source from farmers with a shared value for quality, sustainability, and love for our beautiful environment. We have done extensive research sourcing "only the very best" for our little ones.

How important is good nutrition to child development, sleep, and behavior?

I have always been a believer you need to fuel your body with quality food in order for it to run properly. This mantra is even more applicable to our children and goes for the food you feed your baby from the early days. Your baby should be developing a palate for a variety of real flavor and quality food from the very beginning. A diet high in sugar, artificial ingredients, pesticides, and added fats and salts will ultimately affect your baby/child's overall development. A well-nourished baby will excel in many areas of development from better sleep habits to cognitive development.

Your company was very successful and then you decided to stop, what happened?

The first two years of operations were designed to research the marketplace and clearly understand the opportunity and our market. In February 2008, Baby Gourmet had reached a point where the demand far exceeded the supply and we could no longer keep up with our customer base's needs. We had already expanded our commercial kitchen twice and were not prepared to build a full processing facility for the local market. The market had proven itself and I saw a bigger picture. I made the operational decision to discontinue local production in order to focus on the national commercialization of the brand. As a mother of two, I could not work in the business and strategically plan for the growth congruently. I opted to focus my energy on the bigger picture.

How did your business planning differ from when you launched the company to the break after two years?

When the initial concept came to mind in October 2005, my business planning was extremely conservative and primarily geared towards a Western Canadian expansion. After two years of direct sales, the financial projections tripled and it was obvious the original plan was blown out of the water; the opportunity was much larger than I had anticipated. I never hesitated to believe this brand could be anything less than an international success and started to build the business plan geared towards this vision.

Who did you enlist to support your growth? How important is it to an entrepreneur to build the right kind of infrastructure for her growing business?

For me it was imperative to enlist the right individuals to assist in building my dreams. I am a firm believer in the quality of the team as a whole over the quality of the individual. Right from the beginning I enlisted my sister [Jill Vos], as a key member, to join me on this venture. Over six months I enlisted a highly skilled operational team of four with proven success in execution. I will always credit my personal and company success to the people who supported me by joining in this journey. I could not ask for a better team of people to work with every day, they make success even sweeter. I have built an incredible infrastructure within the organization, which is mandatory in the success of execution.

It is critical for any entrepreneur to look inside, understand what [he or she] can bring to the table, and what someone else can bring. Put your ego aside and bring in people to fill those gaps. I have seen it so many times where people think they can do it all, they end up working on day-to-day operations and not on strategic growth.

How exciting is it to see your business grow from something local to something international?

I have always envisioned this transition, so to see it come to fruition makes me even more of a believer. I love my job, I believe in the cause, and I am passionate about every aspect of this company, and so to do something I feel so strongly about and see success is an incredible feeling. We still have a long way to go but I believe we will reach our optimal goal and enjoy every minute of the journey.

What have been some of your major successes and challenges?

Challenges:

- Balancing work and home life (the hardest). It is difficult to be all to everyone, so finding balance between work, family, and "me time" is challenging.

- The learning curve of entering the food-processing and manufacturing industry. We had to learn everything from food science to engineering.

- Deadlines being pushed back. I was told whatever time line and however much money you think you will need, to double it.

- Getting back up when you have been kicked down. This experience is a complete ride; one day is a high, the next a low. Overcoming the mental and emotional strain of this ride can be challenging at times.

Successes:

- Building a successful and recognizable brand in the marketplace.

- Discovering my passion and being able to work on it every day.

- Finding and securing my execution team.

- Working with a fantastic manufacturer to produce our formulations and develop the best baby food products on the market.

- Locating and sourcing the best ingredients.

- Tasting our mass-produced formulations for the first time and loving them!

- Raising $1.8 million for our expansion.

You work with your sister; what is it like working with a family member? Any tips?

Don't do it! (Just kidding!) Like any close relationship it has its ups and downs. It is very hard work and the communication lines need to be open. Because you are family, there are ties that can never be severed, which can make things difficult. My sister and I are complete opposites, which we have acknowledged and made work for us. Working with family can be very difficult. You need to determine your roles early in the process, set goals together, and ensure you are completely on the same path and wave of thinking. If you are on a different page and you recognize this too late in the game then it becomes a power struggle. My advice is to do your due diligence beforehand and keep in mind this is a business and nothing should be taken personally.

What tips would you offer a woman considering building a business?

I would suggest someone dig deep and really understand the commitment it takes to be an entrepreneur. Itemize a risk analysis and determine if you are willing and able to take all the risks that come along with this role. Risks include financial, time commitment, emotional pressures, etc. Once you have concluded you are a natural-born leader willing and able to handle a bumpy ride, then you need to research your concept and build a solid plan. Be open to bringing in outside resources for execution in any areas you fall short. Most leaders never lack strategy or great ideas, but they do lack execution. Without the proper team to execute your strategies, [plans] have no legs. The last and most important tip I could offer is to believe in yourself and your vision — if you truly believe it, then you will see it!

Finding Money to Go Forward

You have, for the most part, nailed down what your business's mission and vision are, how you will build your product or service base, how you will protect it going forward, and most importantly, you have found out how much money you will need to make all of this happen. You now need to find the money.

1. Going to the Bank

If you plan to go to a bank to fund your business, be prepared to use your own personal credit and personally guarantee your losses until your business is large enough to earn its own credit, have its own assets, and be financially sustainable. To do this, you will need a strong business plan, good credit, and a bank that specializes in serving small businesses that will give you a banker you can depend on.

From my experience, I would recommend going to a bank before considering any other financing option. Banks can usually get you the lowest interest rates if you have good credit, are guaranteed and reputable, and will work with you if you get into trouble. You also will not have to give up a portion of ownership as you would in an investment agreement or partnership opportunity.

Most women assume they will not be able to get any financing from a bank for a variety of different reasons: either they have bad credit, have been out of the workforce for a while on maternity leave or raising their family, or they just make the assumption without looking around. If your business plan has been written properly and has a strong forecast for growth in the future years, there are banks that will work with you.

Ideally, you want to get some kind of business credit established early on in the existence of your business. The sooner you develop a good credit history for the company, the sooner it will be able to get financing without your personal credit or guarantee on the line.

Banks will almost always want to see a strong business plan if you are asking for $50,000 or more; anything less will basically be determined by your personal credit alone. Once you go past that mark, banks will consider financing equipment, receivables, and a variety of other more creative options than a basic business loan. Be prepared for a bank to use your business plan as a way to compare against other successful businesses and their percentages or ratios for things such as labor costs, or raw material costs, to revenue.

They will also consider how many competitors are in your market, how risky your business is and the industry it is in, and debt service or how much money you have coming in to service the debt you are acquiring.

Having a personal relationship with my banker has saved me dozens of times. In my early years as an entrepreneur, and in my experience founding a charity, not only did I build a relationship with my banker on a business level, but it developed into a friendship as well. In the early days of working with government funding, the bank was able to review our contracts and help us with bridge financing when we were waiting on a payment. Going forward, that bank ended up donating to the charity because I had the personal relationship with the banker who took it to her head office and championed our cause.

Although you do not want to acquire credit you don't need for your business, the advice for entrepreneurs to look for financing when times are good, is true. If you have a lot of money in the bank, and a lot of contracts, book an appointment with your banker to review your current financials and see if it will put a line of credit in place for rainy days or an unplanned opportunity. If you don't currently have a bank that supplies you with a banker who manages your business needs, find a bank that will. You may need to interview a few to get the right one, but they are out there.

Another benefit to working with a bank, and more importantly a banker that understands your needs, is that it can help you if you get into trouble. If, unexpectedly, you become cash strapped, you can speak with your lender about deferring a payment, making an interest-only payment, or restructuring your debt. In 2009, many banks set up strategies like these to support their customers. The key is to contact them and work out a deal before you get behind. Unfortunately, many entrepreneurs wait too long until they recognize they are in deep trouble, hoping things will get better. On the one hand, I think this is a personality trait that makes an entrepreneur — the ability to persevere through the toughest of situations and come out on top. On the other hand, it gets a lot of young entrepreneurs into trouble and causes them to wait too long before being aggressive about changing their game plan. Make sure you have the kind of relationship with your banker where you can connect with him or her to mention what you are facing and that you need some support to come through to the other side.

2. Finding a Business Partner

"I love having a partner to bounce ideas off of and problem-solve with. I think double the brain power better serves our clients."

— Andrea Tumato, Woodcreek Business Solutions Ltd.

Finding a partner is sometimes easier than finding investment from a professional firm or credit from a bank. What I see more often than not is two or more friends establishing a business together because they like each other. This can work, especially from a support standpoint, but clear definitions need to be laid out in order to be successful. Each partner needs to have a clear understanding of their roles, the share structure, their voting power, and the direction of the company as well as how they can get out when the time comes. Do not make the mistake of not outlining these things in writing before going into the relationship. If you do not want to pay the legal fees, use the forms on CD kit *Partnership Agreement*, which is also published by Self-Counsel Press. However, you should always have a lawyer look over any agreement you create.

"Our partnership has developed over time, just like our business. Initially, we did everything together — each decision was discussed and decided. After a while, the tasks seemed to divide

fairly naturally based on our strengths and interests. One of us is crazy about marketing and the other loves to read and develop courses. One of us loves to write and the other talks to lots of people, finding out what is happening and generating business. We both work with parents via courses, presentations, and coaching. We share media interviews as well. We talk regularly and keep each other up-to-date with upcoming business opportunities, new clients, and, of course, we do our visionary planning together. We decided at the very beginning that we would not count every minute of work each of us did but rather trust that we were each working about the same amount of time, in varying capacities. This fluctuates, but we believe that it all works out in the end. We split the company's income equally.

Our partnership's greatest strength is the importance of our friendship, which is based on honesty. We know each of us and our families is more important than the business itself. Even though it can be uncomfortable, we talk to each other when we disagree and work through the problem. When we still can't decide, we come back to the overall vision and values of the company and work in that direction. We trust each other a lot and know that we both have the company's best interest at heart. If either of us is adamantly opposed to something, it won't happen, but we are both open to the great things that will happen to our company and will usually give something a try if it is something in which the other believes."

— Julie Freedman Smith, Parenting Power™

If this business is really your dream, be wary when choosing a partner. It may benefit you to keep 100 percent of your company going forward. Be sure you want to get into this relationship before signing on the dotted line.

"I decided to take on a partner in my third year of business. I needed some money to grow the company and I needed the help of a partner for day-to-day operations. My best friend was immediately interested. We signed a partnership agreement — something standard — and had a lawyer take a quick look at it.

A year later we had a falling out, we started to not get along, and we didn't see the same future for the company. She wanted to invest more money to grow it and I had no money to invest. She came from wealth; I had the complete opposite in terms of financing options. We had a shotgun clause written into our original agreement. If she wanted out, I offered her a certain amount of money, or she had to come up with the same amount of money and I would walk away.

About six months after things became really bad between us, she approached me with a shotgun offer for $50,000. I had to either pay her $50,000 or she would pay me $50,000 to walk. I did not have $50,000, nor could I raise it quickly — she knew that and took advantage. I ended up walking away from the business I had launched and was the CEO of, for $50,000. I recently had an accountant look at the financials; he thinks my shares would have been worth well over $100,000."

— Constantine, New York, New York

In the businesses I have established that have had partners, my most difficult times came when we had a dispute that involved the following:

- ❦ When one person felt like she was contributing more time and work than the other.

- ❦ When the company hit financially difficult times and partners needed to invest more dollars and were not willing or able to.

- ❦ When there was a dispute that we could not come to an agreement on and we were both 50/50 owners.

My advice to you if you do go down the path of taking on a partner is to draw up an agreement prior to starting and have it reviewed by a lawyer. Know how you will resolve disputes in a stalemate, what responsibilities each partner has, how the responsibilities will be evaluated, how you will get out if you need to, how you will get the other partner out if needed. Make sure you both have the same goals and aspirations for the growth of the company.

As women, we often do not say the things that need to be said because we are afraid of hurting the other person's feelings. Unfortunately, feelings get hurt, and things need to be said in order to be successful. If you are not comfortable saying, "you are not pulling your weight," or "I can't work with you anymore" then do not go into a partnership.

In my latest partnership I have chosen a partner with a big personality. She is brilliant, successful, and makes good choices. I have learned a lot from her. We both challenge each other on a regular basis. I have a tendency to enjoy a good debate and to a certain degree, a fight. I feel exhilarated and energized, and I think our relationship comes out better in the end. It wasn't until recently that she told me how hard it was for her to get used to the debates. She said she felt like an abused wife sometimes. It took hearing that to realize that I needed to learn to listen as well as speak my mind. Listening and making sure she feels comfortable during a dispute is something I have to continuously work on and watch. Just when I think I have it all figured out, I realize that learning opportunities never end!

2.1 Negotiating the partnership agreement

"I knew going into the recession that in order to survive, I needed more access to cash. I chose a partner who was not very business savvy, nor particularly smart or driven in order to partner with. What she lacked in business skill she made up for in money. We have a great relationship but I definitely led the direction of the company. She sometimes feels I only wanted her for the money; she is right — that is true. This is business, not a friendship."

— Anonymous

A partnership agreement is a legal document and it can be complex, especially when a dispute arises. I have asked lawyer Esther S. Chung of Chung Law Corporation to provide her opinion, as follows in the rest of this section.

The biggest concern with partnerships, whether it is general, limited, or limited liability, is to protect oneself from being liable for the unauthorized acts of partners. Generally, a partner may bind the partnership into any contract or incur a liability for the partnership even if the person wasn't authorized to do so, as long as the third party involved was not aware that the partner was acting outside of her authority. For this reason, a person entering into a partnership needs to concern herself with not just the mechanics of the partnership (i.e., contribution, profit sharing, involvement), but also with ways by which potential liability may be reduced:

- How to remove partners.

- How to leave a partnership, including indemnity from the remaining partners.

- When to dissolve a partnership.

- What to do if a dispute arises.

- The right for each partner to inspect and inquire into the activities of the partnership. By putting into place a method that gives partners the right to identify problems, remove a problematic partner, or to leave if others are acting irresponsibly, they may be able to cut the ties of liability associated with a partnership before it is too late.

One other clause that should also be contemplated is a spousal release clause, whereby the spouses of each partner release their claim to the partnership property and agrees to obtain their equalization of the marital property from other assets. In some areas, the rule of thumb is that a spouse is not entitled to business property, unless the spouse has made a direct or indirect contribution to the business property. Oftentimes, a homemaker can assert that his or her services to the keeping of the home and children permitted the other spouse to focus his or her attention to business, thereby making an indirect contribution. While courts will try to find other assets from which to equalize a spouse's entitlement (with or without a partnership agreement), if no other assets exist to collect from, then the divorcing partner may need to withdraw partnership in order to pay out the spouse. If this partner is a key contributor, it may ultimately break up the partnership. In this regard, especially if any of the spouses of the partners are homemakers or work from home, partners should ensure that no more than half of the combined assets of the couple are being invested in the partnership, and if so, they should try to find a way that would keep the partnership viable (e.g., spouse agrees to become a limited partner of the company, or to make a loan to the partnership for the shortfall).

Between strangers, friends, and families, the biggest difference is in the degree of trust between partners. Along with the degree of trust comes the corresponding degree of leeway that is often assumed by trusted members, and the potential for hurt feelings that prevent partners from resolving issues (hoping it will resolve itself). For example, in a family partnership, the children may assume that they may reduce the work load from time to time, since mom and dad will "understand." It's hard to make a clear distinction between friends and family because some relationships are stronger or weaker than others. It is often the case that when a friendship breaks down, partners may start pointing fingers no differently than strangers, whereas family members are more likely to withdraw and avoid going after each other, all the while severely damaging the family relationship.

I find friends, but more so families, to be less willing to spell out each other's rights, responsibilities, and protective mechanisms because they don't want to believe it may be required, or they don't want to hurt the other's feelings. Friends and families, even for relatively small and simple ventures, may wish to see a lawyer to receive "initial advice," so that the lawyer may be the one to suggest and encourage protective clauses (if they are unable to bring themselves to say it themselves, the lawyer can do it for them).

Aside from the difficulties arising from the nature of the relationship, family members may need to take extra precaution to draw clear distinctions between each member's contributions. Especially where parents are making most of the financial contribution (as they often do), even if parents ultimately mean to give it all to their children anyway, they should clearly hang on to their shares until such a time comes. Again, if this is not made clear, misunderstanding between family members can lead to a breakdown of the venture as well as the relationship. Another thing to consider is the protection of the family business from the ex-spouses of the children. If it is clear that the parents hold the larger share, it will be more difficult for ex-spouses to try and claim a part of that as the child-partner's share.

Liability includes both existing problems and the risk of problems. For example, a poorly maintained business premises may not yet be an existing claim of personal injury, but certainly presents a risk of such claim in the future. The poor state of the business premises in that case is a liability (though they may not be liable to anyone at the moment). Except for certain regulated professions (e.g., lawyers), shareholders of a corporation are protected from personal liability. This means that, if the company cannot repay its debts, fulfill its end of a contract, or has caused injury (physical or financial) to another, the third party can get repaid or compensated out of the company's property only. If at any time, a company cannot meet its liability, the creditors may pick the company clean and the shortfall will be their loss (not the shareholders). There are a few exceptions to shareholders' liabilities. For example, if a company is about to be insolvent, and shareholders sold off the company property and divided up the profits, the creditors may go after the shareholders, but only for that portion. Or, shareholders are often directors, and as a director, that person can be still held liable for unpaid wages to employees. To avoid risk of any shareholder's (or director's) liability when the company is in trouble, it is advisable that they seek a lawyer's advice to limit it as much as possible. For example, the lawyer will advise to pay the employees first, and then advise as to how to pay out the various creditors to avoid being deemed in preference of one creditor or another.

Partnerships and corporations are governed by each state or province, and as such, should consult the state or province's applicable laws before making final decisions. As for family law, it is the general concept that a spouse has the right to the combined success of the relationship.

3. Factoring

"We are a small business and we needed funds to take care of our day-to-day expenses. As immigrants with no background in Canada and not enough in the bank, this was a big challenge for us. When a company pays us, it can take up to 60 days to receive the money. Factoring helps tide us over during that period until we receive the money. It has been working well for me and I'm happy with our decision."

— Kajal Bahadur, 21 Zeta Inc.

Factoring is an option to businesses with a large accounts receivable but with not a lot of cash flow. A perfect example would be an administrative support company for oil and gas operations. Typically its invoices would be paid within 30 to 60 days. The administrative company needs to pay its payroll every two weeks. To avoid a cash-flow crunch, the company will in effect, sell its accounts receivable to a "factor" who will give the company cash in return for a percentage. The factor will then go to the company with the invoice and collect on it. If you find a reliable factor to do this with, the factor can, in effect, become a key financial piece to the growth of your company.

Be careful when choosing a factor. You need to know that it will then be in direct contact with your client. Be sure that the factor will deal with the client in a professional manner. Make sure you choose a company that is reputable and has worked in your industry.

4. Professional Investors

"I knew if I was to go to market for investment, my business would need to be in impeccable order. I could not take the risk of not having my business plan in top notch shape, having my financials in order, or having my systems in place. I needed private equity to reach my goals; I was not going to screw it up by not having my ducks in a row."

— Carol, London, Ontario

❦ Despite owning 48 percent of businesses in the USA, women still only receive an average of 4 percent of private equity each year to start new businesses.[1]

❦ Because of this lack of capital, women-owned businesses surpass annual revenues of one million dollars in less than 3 percent of cases.[1]

When you have remortgaged your home, maxed out every credit card, and borrowed from every person who ever said they loved you, and you still need more, you have hit the point where you need to get professional investment. Every entrepreneur comes to a point in his or her career when he or she understands to really take their business to the next level, he or she is going to need some serious cash in order to make it happen. Asking for money can be an intimidating process. In order to be successful, you need to be prepared. If you know you need to start looking for investment dollars, here are the steps you need to take in order to make that happen.

One of the most common questions I get when I am discussing this option to finance is where and how do you find investors? There are a couple of different routes. If you have built a company with a large enough profile and a potential for large growth, I guarantee you, someone is already watching you. Become comfortable attending events and asking people for referrals for investors, or ask who they received their private equity dollars from. There are also websites that can get you connected quickly, but be very cautious — this arrangement and finance option is not for the faint of heart. Don't commit to anything before doing your due diligence on whom the investors are, what they are looking for, and whether they really have the money. Always get references. Once you have found your investor, the work isn't done, be prepared to go forward cautiously.

---

[1] Kim Lavine, *The Mommy Manifesto*, (New Jersey: Wiley, 2009).

You need to understand that in order to get a large chunk of cash to go forward, you may need to sell 50 percent or more of your shares depending on how much money is needed. This is the decision of having a small piece of something huge or a big piece of something that never really got off the ground. Also, investors are not going to just hand over a large sum of their money without being able to control the use of it. So before going out with a proposal for money, make sure you know your bottom line in what you are willing to give up before signing a unanimous shareholder's agreement. An angel investment is a financial arrangement, not a charitable donation. Just because they call themselves "angels" does not mean they are. If you take on an investor, you take on a boss.

You need to know that investors will not invest money so that you can clear up your outstanding debt that you have invested in the business. They only want to work with entrepreneurs with as much to lose — proportionally — as they have. Also, don't expect them to fund losses; this money is all about going forward and driving your business to make the profit margins that give them a high return on investment.

Although you may really like these people and they may really like you, when things go south for your business, their first and only priority is their money. They will do whatever it takes to get it back, even if that means terminating you in your current role and taking drastic measures that you may not agree with. Make sure when negotiating your contract, that you have included options to include board members of your choosing and the investor's approval so that someone objective can support the best interests of the company in hard times.

You will need to learn to say some very difficult things to sometimes intimidating people. One of the best pieces of advice I ever got was to buy the book *Crucial Conversations: Tools for Talking When the Stakes Are High* (McGraw-Hill, 2002) by Kerry Patterson, Joseph Grenny, Ron McMillan, and Al Switzler. This was an extremely influential book for me and taught me to see where I was not speaking my truth about certain situations.

I had become partners with an investment firm where one member was a real bully. She would raise her voice, slap the table, and on every email she had to include about as many exclamation marks as babies have dirty diapers. She was like an angry, wounded bear that would stomp around yelling and intimidating people until she got her way. I was always waiting for her head to spin around and pea soup to spew from her mouth. I had to practice and practice and practice some more, keeping my voice calm, hearing her perspective and then speaking from the person on the front lines on what needed to be done. It was the book *Crucial Conversations* that taught me to stand up to her in a classy way and also to say that I chose to no longer be treated poorly by her.

Difficult conversations that make your blood pressure skyrocket are essential to being the leader of any organization. Just as an aside, although that bully was a real pill to deal with, she got things done. Although, I would never treat people as she did, and I have learned to say quickly when things are bothering me and to turn my mind away from the thought that this person may not like me if I say I am disappointed, upset, or angry at what he or she has done. That grumpy bear has really made a difference in my communication skills in every aspect of my life. Even though I learned a lot, I just don't want to work with people like that anymore; it wasn't worth the money she invested.

When making a pitch to an investment firm for dollars, you usually submit a cover letter with the amount you are looking for, up-to-date financials, financials from the beginning of your business, your current team members, a proper business plan that includes a marketing plan, and a detailed description of how much money you need and how the money will be used. You can be creative in how you present this information; in fact, I encourage you to be. If I have learned anything about this process, it is that an investor is more interested in investing in you as entrepreneur and your passion for this business than in the perfection of a business plan.

"A lot of these people that have made their millions on business models from twenty years ago are just desperately trying to remain relevant."

— Kim Lavine, entrepreneur and author

Understand that just because someone is wealthy, does not mean he or she knows what the best direction is for your company. In my case, the women I worked with became wealthy many years earlier on business models that either did not apply to what I had been doing or were not relevant because they were so outdated.

"In the end, I knew I had to make a decision, would I own a little of a lot, or a lot of something really little. I had to focus on what I really wanted to do and that was to build a company focused on the promotion of play and physical activity; in order to do that, I had to choose to sell a portion of my company to find the right investment team to support me in that dream."

— Traci Costa, Peekaboo Beans

As you go down the route toward signing a unanimous shareholder's agreement with a professional investment firm, an interesting place to start is Lawrence Lenihan's "The Funding Bill of Rights" (http://lawrencelenihan.wordpress.com/the-funding-bill-of-rights). Although not a legal document, it gives the entrepreneur a clear perspective on what a venture capitalist is looking for and what some of the risks for the entrepreneur are.

I was recently speaking with a client of mine who was one year into her relationship with her investment team. I casually asked how she felt about answering to and being evaluated by this team and whether or not she ever worried about being terminated or placed in the basement for research and development instead of being front and center as the CEO. She answered, "Can they do that?" Well, yes, in most instances they can and they will. From my research, more than 80 percent of entrepreneurs who take on venture capital dollars are no longer the CEO within 24 months. This is obviously not an issue if your exit strategy includes leaving within the next 24 months; it becomes a problem when you were hoping to stay.

Choosing the right investment partner isn't easy. In one of my businesses, I chose a couple of women that were new to investing but wanted to support the growth of women's businesses. What I was too naïve to ask were the following questions:

- How will you be involved in my business? Will you only be available to me at board meetings or do you want to be more involved in day-to-day operations? What do you expect of me at board meetings? These are the things I need from you:

  - Investment of dollars

  - Investment of consultation time

  - Inclusion and introduction to your network

- How many people will be on the board of directors that will be established with this investment? How many will be objective and at arm's reach from either of us?

It is so important that you begin to look for investment dollars before you are desperate for money, but choosing the wrong partner will almost certainly be the precursor to disaster.

4.1 Negotiating a shareholder's agreement

"We hit really hard times financially with the recession, no one was buying. I couldn't sell a thing; my staff couldn't sell a thing. There was no money and my investors were no longer willing to spend money to fund losses. There was not enough money for my salary. Within six months I was personally desperate. I told my investors I would have to be paid or else I couldn't continue. They refused to invest any more funds into covering a loss. I refused to work without being paid. They terminated me from my own company; I was still a shareholder, but one with no power. I ended up suing my own company. It was horrible."

— Anonymous, Dallas, Texas

Protecting yourself from situations like these is not easy and it must be done in the early stages of negotiating your unanimous shareholder's agreement. You must have your own lawyer who specializes in this kind of agreement and who can protect your interests, especially if you are not in an equitable financial position.

Professional investors are often silent investors (with non-voting shares) and have nothing to do with the actual operation of the company. It is often the professional investors who will demand or require a unanimous shareholder's agreement so that they have some control over some of the company's decisions to ensure the company is run properly (to their standards). As they will be the ones asking for the unanimous shareholder's agreement, it is best to see what they want, and ask a lawyer how it may affect the company.

You will need to agree on the board of directors that includes others as well as you and your investment team. The following sections cover other terms you will need to agree with before you sign on with investors.

Because you will often be signing away more than half of your company, I decided to bring in our trusty lawyer, Esther S. Chung from Chung Law Corporation, to help provide some clarity on this topic. Her expertise is provided in the following sections (**4.1a** to **4.1h**).

4.1a Executive management agreement

All companies with more than one shareholder should consider having the shareholders enter into a shareholder's agreement. No matter what country you reside in, the principles of a shareholder's agreement are the same. Before going on this topic, a "unanimous shareholder's agreement" is a special term used to designate an agreement designed to re-apportion powers within a company.

Unanimous shareholder's agreements are most often used where shareholders with very small interest wish to protect themselves from the powers of the larger shareholders. For example, shareholders still have control over the company by voting on the directors and some corporate decisions; however, most of these require only a majority vote, and other special resolutions will require a "special resolution" vote (each province has a default percentage required, unless the articles indicate otherwise). For those who hold only a small percentage of the shares, they may be powerless if the other shareholders are in agreement.

A unanimous shareholder's agreement generally contains provisions so that certain decisions must have the unanimous consent of all shareholders. A unanimous shareholder's agreement is often not an issue where there are a small number of shareholders all with close-to-equal shareholdings. A unanimous shareholder's agreement is also considered outside of the normal course of a company's procedure, and as such, shareholders should have a particular power-related concern that they would like to address before deciding to put together this type of agreement.

The requirement for unanimous consent can be either for decisions normally left to shareholders, or for decisions left to directors. Depending on the jurisdiction, however, the decision-making powers of the directors cannot be assumed through a shareholder's agreement, but must be included in the articles (which is amended by a shareholder's resolution, the required percentage depending on the type of powers being amended and the jurisdiction of the company).

As the considerations needed to be made regarding unanimous shareholder's agreements is different for each jurisdiction, and as the concern addressed by the agreement is quite serious, if power-related issues are of a concern to a shareholder, she should seek the advice of a lawyer to ensure that the rights she seeks to protect are adequately protected.

Shareholder's agreements are only effective if every shareholder signs on to the deal. As the share structure will determine each shareholder's right to dividends, and the decision-making process is addressed by stat-ute and articles (or sometimes unanimous shareholder's agreement), the shareholder's agreement focuses more on what the shareholders expect from each other, and how to resolve problems.

Some of the common topics in a shareholder's agreement are as follows:

- Identifying the business of the corporation
- Contributions of the shareholders
- Operation and control of the corporation
- Restrictions on issue and transfers of shares
- Financing
- Mechanisms to remove a shareholder, or to leave the company
- Mechanisms for the right to purchase future shares
- Mechanisms for the right to sell shares
- What to do on the death of a shareholder
- Life insurance
- Family law matters (similar to the way it was discussed under partnerships)
- Limitation of liability

4.1b Contribution

If any of the shareholders are going to be actively involved in working for the company (as opposed to the company hiring outside employees), then the shareholders should agree on the scope of work expected, and how they are going to be remunerated. It can get quite awkward if a shareholder agrees to provide a key service for the business, and the other shareholders try to pay that person as little as possible for his or her time (or, having that key person demand too much).

If the shareholders agree that they will take turns running the com-pany part time (one month each, split evenings and weekends, etc.), the method of division should also be addressed. You don't want to strain the company dynamic because someone always wants to take the sum-mer off, for example.

4.1c Mechanisms to remove a shareholder or to leave the company

Shareholders should also put in a mechanism to either remove a shareholder, or to leave the company with fair compensation. How this can be done depends on the dynamics of the shareholders.

If it is just two people with equal shares, they can often agree to put in a "shotgun" clause. In that case, if any one determines that they should go their separate ways, the shotgun clause determines who gets to leave for how much, and who gets to keep the company. Usually, a shareholder can submit in writing that the clause will be put into effect, and offering to sell or buy out the other person for a specific sum. The other shareholder must accept the offer or reverse the offer. For example, if A tells B that she will sell her shares for $50,000, and B feels that A has named too high of a price, then B can always make A buy out B for the exact same price. By using a shotgun clause, shareholders can avoid going through business evaluation (the fair market evaluation is built-in by nature).

Where the shareholders are two couples with equal shares, it can also work well, but the husband and wife must leave as a team.

With more than two groupings of shareholders with equal shareholdings, the shotgun clause is difficult to implement. In that case, there should be in place a mechanism to remove a shareholder or to demand that a shareholder be bought out. The right to be removed or bought out can be under any circumstance, or specific. There should also be a method in which to determine the buy-out price (either by business evaluation or by a calculation based on the financial statement).

4.1d Operation and control

Shareholders can also agree ahead of time as to how they will vote in the future. For example, shareholders can agree that A be elected president one year, B the next, and C the next (or name directors). A unanimous shareholder's agreement may also be included as a part of this section.

If shareholders desire to limit the operation and control of a particular shareholder, it should also be set out in a shareholder's agreement. For example, if in a restaurant, one is the chef and the other manages the business, the chef may want to ensure that the other has no say as to the menu selection or the management of the kitchen staff.

4.1e Share restrictions

For companies held by friends and family, it may be undesirable for one shareholder to sell her share to a complete stranger. Shareholders can agree ahead of time that shareholders cannot sell to others without the unanimous consent of all other shareholders (they may instead be bought out by other shareholders, or a method can be built in by which the company will buy back the shares).

Shareholders may not want shares to be issued such that the ratio of shareholdings are affected or diluted. Restrictions can prevent new shares being issued without unanimous consent.

4.1f Financing

Companies can obtain corporate loans, or may borrow money from shareholders (shareholder's loans). Corporate loans may have high rates of interest, so shareholders may agree to loan the company money. In such a case, unless the shareholders agree that loans must be made and paid out equally, the interest rate should be specified so that the other shareholders are not required to foot a high interest rate (especially if only one shareholder is the company's only available source of financing).

4.1g Death of a shareholder and insurance

When a person dies, her executor will take the shares as trustee of the estate, and the shares can be passed on to the deceased's beneficiaries. The involvement of an outsider, as it essentially appears, can disrupt business. It is desirable to buy out the deceased person's share immediately so as to minimize the disruption. If the other shareholders are sufficiently wealthy, they may bind themselves to purchase the deceased person's share equally. However, if not all the shareholders have access to enough funds, companies often take out life insurance on each shareholder with the company as the designated beneficiary (for an amount sufficient to buy out that person's shares). In such a case, the company receives the insurance proceeds and uses it to purchase the deceased's shares. Depending on who the shareholders are, this situation can be resolved quite creatively. For example, if it is a family corporation, there may be a specific provision for the mother or father such that the surviving spouse has the right to purchase the other spouse's shares for $1, or if there is no surviving spouse, that the children each get the right to purchase an equal share of the deceased's shares for $1 each. Ultimately, the arrangement will depend on if the grown children have children of their own who may step up in the family business (very situation specific).

4.1h Limitation of liability and indemnification

In general, if you guarantee a loan on behalf of another and you are called on to pay, the guarantor has the right to go after the debtor to get that money repaid (still problematic, as the debtor usually doesn't have the money if it comes to this). If shareholders give personal guarantees on corporate loans, the lender usually places a clause so that he or she may go after anyone (who is convenient to him or her) for the entire amount. In such a case, the shareholder who pays only has the right to go after the company. As such, in order to prevent a shareholder from having to pay off the company's debts on her own, shareholders can agree to indemnify each other according to their shareholdings.

Shareholders are protected from the company's liabilities; however, if a company enters into trouble, it can ultimately cost the shareholder. For example, if a company must pay out someone, that reduces the company's net earnings, reducing each person's dividends. Or if the company becomes insolvent, then the shareholders may never recover their investments (or the value of the assets). Shareholders can agree that, where a company's loss is caused by a shareholder (the "causation" aspect should be clearly defined; for example, if a shareholder performs an unauthorized act), then that shareholder must reimburse the company for the losses incurred (thereby not harming the other shareholders).

Note: Where a company is the beneficiary of the shareholder's agreement (e.g., life insurance, indemnity), the company should be made a party to the contract.

> "The best thing I ever did was to buy back my company. I want to encourage all women to go out and raise capital — that is half the battle — the other half of the battle is in the boardroom. You have to remain committed to being a leader."
>
> — Kim Lavine, entrepreneur and author

5. Finding the Right Investor

Finding the right investor for your business is a bit like finding a spouse, except there is no sex and the divorce rate is higher among the invested! Every entrepreneur comes to a place where he or she needs to decide how the business will continue. Will it continue along the same path of mediocrity with a level line of growth or will he or she take the plunge, borrow someone else's money, and really skyrocket the business?

In a perfect world, borrowing someone else's money seems like an optimal choice for growing your business. Unfortunately it is not as easy as it sounds. TV shows such as *Shark Tank* and *Dragons' Den* show an interesting perspective, like being a fly on the wall during the pitch of a passionate entrepreneur. More often it shows the desperation of entrepreneurs when they have reached their financial threshold. It is a bit like being at the school dance when the awkward girl stares with longing for a boy, any boy, to rescue her.

Ideally, once you have decided to go to market for investment, you should play the field, look for interested parties, and interview them. Your opportunity for them is just as meaningful as theirs is to you.

In my experience in working with investors, they are all different and have different views. What it comes down to is always money and getting a return on the investment. Don't plan for them to consider your needs, wants, or priorities. This is a financial relationship only — both you and the investor need to understand this.

I remember distinctly being in a board meeting with my investors, when one said, "You seem to only think of us as an ATM machine, that our only worthwhile contribution to the company is money." I replied with platitudes, saying that I was grateful for their investment and that I had learned a lot from them. What I should have said was, "That was your role in coming on board, you were only needed for financial investment, and your business experience has not proven helpful in this situation." This is where you need to have those clear responsibilities laid out before you ever sign on the dotted line. It shouldn't have to be discussed one or two years into the arrangement.

A girlfriend came out of a prospective interview recently and said, "I was just so unimpressed. I was expecting them to have all of the answers, [but] instead, their ideas made me uncomfortable — they were so far off base from what I needed. They obviously had money and had been successful in other industries but did not understand mine."

Luckily she was not desperate and had the financial capacity to keep looking. She trusted her gut and that she knew her business more than the people on the other side of the table. When going to market, you need to consider what it is you need:

- Is it only money?

- Is it money plus infrastructure to grow?

- Is it influence, networking opportunities, and infrastructure?

- Have the investors done this before?

- Do the investors have references you can speak with that have been with them past the 24-month mark?

If I was to ever work with investors again, which I am not sure I would, I would want them not only for their financial commitment, but I would want them to support the growth of infrastructure as the first item on the priority list. In all of the interviews I conducted during the eight months I researched for this book, the women that were successful with investors were those that had the investors, themselves, and others on the board of directors; infrastructure to support the entrepreneur was the first priority; and those that felt comfortable enough and strong enough to speak up and defend ideas at the board level.

6. Managing Your Money

"I think everyone has a cash-flow crunch right now. You have to do more with less. You have to bootstrap in new ways every day."

— Kim Lavine, entrepreneur and author

After losing my first big business and selling my last, I have spent a lot of time on a postmortem of each. What would I do differently if I had to do it again? One of the most consistent answers I get (from myself and from others I have interviewed in similar situations) is that I would have managed my cash differently. I would have spent less, and kept track more. Obviously, experience matters. I now know how to budget properly and what I need to spend money on. I know how to do more on my own without paying someone else to do it for me, and I know how to evaluate the effectiveness of my business decisions on a regular basis. That being said, I am not sure there will ever be too much cash for a business to manage, so every penny counts.

The following are some things to consider. If you don't have a solid understanding of bookkeeping, make sure you budget for a bookkeeper or an accountant to help guide you through the budgeting and spending process.

6.1 Understand cash flow

If your definition of cash flow is flawed, you will never be in a comfortable enough financial situation to grow. Just because you have $100,000 in receivables does not mean you will have enough in the bank to cover your payroll. Cash flow is the comparison of when you expect to see your revenue come in versus when you have to pay out your expenses and what that ebb and flow looks like when charted.

Follow some basic cash-flow management rules:

- Try to build a "war chest" of money for when times get tight or something happens and you need it. Relying on credit cards is an expensive way to finance a business and cards are usually secured in your personal name.

- Always be thinking ahead to new revenue. Never rely on your current accounts to stay active.

- Cash is King so treat it with respect and hire someone to teach you how to use it wisely.

- You must keep your accounting books constantly up-to-date and have cash-flow projections. You must always know where you stand financially in order to make smart decisions and move forward.

- Make sure you are taking care of your customers so that they will continue to refer you and rehire you or be repeat buyers in the years to come.

- Know what your cash balance is now and what it will be six months from now. Do your day-to-day work but keep your eyes focused on the future.

6.2 Have a plan for when a cash crisis strikes

"Who doesn't have cash-flow issues at one time or another? I started with nothing but a dream and a whole hell of a lot of confidence. I hustled, and I mean hustled, to make it work. I bartered, I juggled, and I put things on credit that had no business being on credit. However, I continually set aside money instead of just blindly pouring it all back into the business. It's crucial to have security before expansion. You need a safety net to get you through the lean months without hyperventilating. For me, that meant being the interior designer who didn't own a stick of furniture. That meant no vacations for nearly ten years. That meant celebrating media successes with a PlayStation marathon and a bottle of wine instead of a glamorous evening out.

There's no magic formula. What I would spend my money on might make your heart jump but what you deem necessary might seem like a giant waste to me. You have to make decisions that are comfortable for you and your goals, not what any official guidelines tell you to do. Chasing predictability will only make you crazy; do what you have to do but do it while you're busting your ass."

— Erica Swanson, *Erica Swanson Design*

What is your plan for when a cash crisis strikes? If you don't have a plan you had better find one because you can be sure there will be tight times. It is the divine right of every entrepreneur to know the lean times intimately.

"I didn't finance my business as much as I inventoried it with product that I had accumulated over the years but never actually used. I grew the business by purchasing supplies with credit cards. That was a huge mistake. When I lost my full-time job and the show-clothing market took a temporary dive, I was in serious financial trouble. So, yes, I struggle with cash flow every day. I am overcoming the issue with better sales (changed target market), better advertising, and [I'm] expanding where my clothing and supplies can be seen. I also improved the website and the shopping cart has helped. I am also taking advantage of social networking such as the Mommy Millionaire chatroom, Facebook, Twitter, and LinkedIn.

I am also becoming known throughout the industry as a place for one-stop shopping. Most of my customers are on short time frames when ordering (we all procrastinate) and my ability to provide what they want with one phone call or stop on my website has meant significant repeat business."

— Pegg Johnson, *Show Clothes Unlimited*

6.3 When tough times hit

"Hey there, Mr. Grumpy Gills. When life gets you down do you wanna know what you've gotta do? Just keep swimming."

— Dori, *Finding Nemo*

I am no stranger to difficult times in business; in fact, sometimes they are enough to make me reconsider the life I have chosen — but only for a moment. For the most part, difficult times for me can be broken down into two categories: financial stress and emotional stress.

Financial stress comes with having a business. It is a fact of life and one that, although it cannot be avoided, it can be limited. I heard Bill Gates speak once about building a war chest of money in case of trouble, always knowing you had it to rely on. I have used this piece of advice often. Just as women are reminded to always have enough money so that they can walk away from a partner at any time, I try to have enough money in a business to fight for my business or myself in that business at any time.

Regardless of who you are or who you have partnered with, it seems to me that whenever money is threatened — be it yours, someone else's, or another business's — lawyers are unleashed. As a matter of principle and financial strategy, I try to only get into a legal battle if all other forms of communication have broken down or if someone else's lawyer comes at me first. For those of you who are new to business, expect to have a situation where you need to sue or you are threatened with a lawsuit. It is just a part of the game.

This is where having an established relationship with a smart lawyer who has your back and is ready to advise quickly and efficiently is so important in the ownership of a business. Even if you never have to let anyone know you have consulted a lawyer, know your rights and the rights of your opponents at all times.

From an emotional perspective, dealing with the stress of a lawsuit, potential breakdown of a partnership, or whatever you may be facing, can be more than you are ready to cope with on your own. When tough times hit, and they will, you must be prepared. Psychologist Janet Miller advises the following:

🛒 When there is stress all around you, it is important to do what you can to eat well; get some exercise; have quality sleep; and have a confidante that you can cry with, scream with, or just be with — someone who knows you (and if you don't want to do this with a friend or family member, then a therapist can be a great option). Meditate, breathe, trust, plan, and focus on what you can control.

🛒 Try to take "time" out of the equation. When we feel rushed and pressured and "under the gun," we often feel in crisis. If we can slow things down, give ourselves time to work things through, think things out, access resources, and listen to our advisors and ourselves, that sense of crisis often dissipates.

❦ Let go of what you cannot control. Time spent worrying about things that are outside of your realm of influence will only increase your stress.

❦ "Be prepared for the worst — then hope for the best." (I don't know who said this, but it's great advice! Wikiquote dates it back to *Seneca's Morals* from 1702.) If I can anticipate the worst-case scenario and get ready for it — imagine myself coping with it, imagine how I will get through it — then I can face that possibility with some confidence in myself, in my own resilience. It takes some of the fear out of it. It means that I am less likely to be afraid to walk through the crisis or avoid taking it on. Once I have confidence in my resiliency, then I can start thinking about the best outcome — what am I hoping for? What would I love to see happen here? What would be the best outcome? I work on envisioning that, on seeing it in my mind, and I hope for it … knowing that I am prepared for the worst, but I am putting my mental energy into hoping for the best. This helps me to stay positive, and having a positive outlook does wonders for our health and well-being.

7. Learn to Negotiate

"The biggest mistake women make in negotiating is assuming the other party has the same wants, needs, and desires as they do and making concessions the other person never even considered. They also worry about being perceived as bitchy or demanding if they speak up for what they really want and giving in far too easily. You can't get upset by standard emotional tactics people use when playing hardball or take things personally.

Be very clear on what you want and why. Know what you would do if you can't come to reasonable terms. Understand the zone of potential agreement and what the conditions are under which you would leave a negotiation, before you even start. Understand the standard strengths and weaknesses the other party has in negotiations and focus on creating a deal that is good for them based on who they are and what they want. Pay attention to the value of the relationship versus the value of the outcome — you don't necessarily need to 'win' every negotiation; that is, get the best deal or the best terms if it means that it will hurt you more in the long run."

— Michelle LaBrosse, PMP, coauthor of
Cheetah Negotiations: How to Get What You Want, Fast

A client I recently took on to revamp her business plan was paying almost full retail prices for a portion of her raw materials for a gift basket franchise. She really enjoyed working with a particular manufacturer, had developed a personal relationship, and didn't know the industry standard of keystone margins. She needed someone who would sell to her at 50 percent of the retail cost — or keystone. She had been told previously by this manufacturer that she did not order in large enough quantities to warrant wholesale costs. Together we went back to the manufacturer and made it clear that we wanted to maintain the relationship but we were no longer willing to pay that cost, especially when we were buying more and more each month.

We researched their competitors and found less expensive options. We went back to the original vendor and mentioned how much we had been quoted for a similar product and asked the vendor to match it. It did and it made a dramatic difference to the bottom line of my client's gifting franchise. From then on, each year, she sought out quotes from each manufacturer who wanted to compete for her business on each piece of raw material and analyzed her spending to make sure that she was paying the smallest amount for her standard of quality.

Even if you have been told that a price is the best a vendor can do, you have not really heard the best price until you decide to take your business elsewhere. Just like you do not attach your identity and self-esteem to your business, you also have to be ruthless when negotiating for your business, despite the fact that you might really like someone personally.

My favorite movie is *The Godfather*, for the simple fact that its most famous and prominent line is: "It's not personal, it's just business." Words the entrepreneurial woman needs to live by.

Case Study: Using Professional Investors

Anonymous, Toronto, Ontario

I was four years into my business when I was approached by an older lady who told me she was a private investor. She asked if I would be interested in selling a portion of my business in order to access funds to grow it much larger. She was friendly (obviously wealthy) and she was attending an event put on by my business. She seemed to know it well.

We booked a meeting to discuss the idea further with her business partner, an accountant. I really liked the accountant, she was in her senior years as well, maybe 70 or so, had grandchildren, and understood what it took to run a business with young children. She had started as a single mom and became successful with her own firm. The other was a bit older, had never had children and was born with a silver spoon in her mouth. She had not had business success but had made major achievements in the charitable community. She also had an edge to her; she seemed to look down her nose at me. Once, when I made a comment about a gourmet chocolatier in our city, she told me, "You don't need any chocolate" (referring to the size of my body). She reminded me of a slave owner, she looked like she would be more comfortable having servants. Later, I would become the person that took the brunt of her nagging, endless criticisms, and temper tantrums.

I knew my business had achieved a certain level of success, most entrepreneurial women knew of me in the community. I also knew a recession was coming, that I was working way too much, and that I really wanted another baby. I had the choice to sell it outright, take on a partner, or take on professional investors.

Because I wasn't ready to sell yet, I chose to take on the professional investors; they had experience, a strong network, and connections to more money if their investment was to run out. It was exciting signing that agreement. It turned out I was their first partner in this business, although one of them had invested before in small companies.

Our first couple of months went well, although I was given an inside look into what my future held. In the first weeks of the agreement, the difficult investor would send multiple messages a day. She would also have these incredible outbursts over email. One in particular referred to a comment I had made about our current government making some potential changes to the maternity leave benefits of entrepreneurs. I had asked our community what they thought of it. She went ballistic, felt that it was going against her political party's platform, and made such a fuss that I ended up having to put something in about her party's political goals in terms of women. It was embarrassing seeing a grown woman act so crazy. I began to wonder if I had sold my soul to the devil.

It got worse from there. A major recession hit, I could not make a sale for the life of me, I had become pregnant (I had discussed this with the investors in advance), and things were becoming strained in the relationship. The partner that was reasonable, that I could easily work with and who I felt could really teach me to grow in my career, was basically missing in action. She would show up for board meetings physically, but she would be typing on her Black-Berry throughout and would not get involved when her business partner started to act like a two-year-old child. It really taught me a lot about conflict conversations, but I felt like the only thing I was learning was how to tame a shrew in a corporate setting.

Things fell apart when the two of them had a major falling out. The reasonable one approached me and let me know she wanted to push out the other. I felt like it was my chance to really go forward — the one person that was holding us back would be gone, there seemed to be light at the end of the tunnel in terms of the recession, and the partner I liked was willing to step up and meet with me weekly to help grow the business. We even went so far as to approach another potential board member and negotiate a potential partnership with her. We were three months into that planning when the original two seemed to just kiss and make up. All of a sudden the shrew was back and she was pissed off that we had tried to oust her. She took it out on me. We had a board meeting where she demanded financials from me, something the accountant said she was handling because I had just had a baby and was overwhelmed with work. It was this crazy moment where the shrew was demanding I produce these financials and the accountant just looked down at her notes and refused to stand up and say she had taken accountability for them. I was at a loss: Did I betray the partner I was hoping to move forward with by saying she had taken it over while the coup was being planned, or did I keep my mouth shut and hope that the shrew walked away with the payment plan the other had originally offered? In the end, she would not accept that plan, she was back for good, and not only that, she wanted to take over operations — supposedly to "help" me.

It was a mess, I was sick that she was involved again, I felt betrayed by the accountant, and we were still trying to recover from a recession. I hadn't taken a full paycheck in months. The shrew on the investment team had said that she would invest no more funds because she was funding losses and because she did not have accurate financials — something the accountant had promised to produce. My marriage was in crisis because we were surviving on credit cards and I was working like a dog. My husband could not understand why I would not stand up to these two women; it came down to me deciding to continue on the emotional rollercoaster and financial ruin by working with the investors or deciding to walk away. I chose to let them know I was leaving, that I wanted to be bought out. We had a board meeting where they said they would resolve the financial issues by bringing me up-to-date in pay within the next two weeks if I stayed. I agreed.

I went home feeling so excited, I committed to my husband that our money would be in within two weeks and that I was going to be working less, that these investors who couldn't get themselves organized had finally decided to step up to the plate and work things out so we could move forward. I thought my prayers had been answered. The next day the meeting minutes were circulated. It included nothing about my back pay, but stated I had resigned, they had accepted the resignation, and that they were taking over operations of the company.

It went from bad to worse and cost me over $10,000 to sort out with lawyers. I look back and realize they were never interested in helping me grow my business; they wanted my business and thought it would be cheaper and easier to just take mine under the pretense of investment and push me out. We were all wrong — a very expensive mistake for me and the investors.

Your Marketing Plan

One of the biggest mistakes I see entrepreneurs make is to fail to properly plan the marketing initiatives for the years ahead. So much focus goes into the development of a great product and its manufacturing, or a great service and its delivery, and very little energy goes in to how to tell a target market about it, if entrepreneurs even know their target market. I think many make the frightening assumption that their product or service will be so great that its growth will just happen — this inevitably ends up in undisciplined spending and disappointment resulting from haphazard attempts to get the word out after a few months and a stale start.

The first thing to consider is the calendar for the year ahead. When do you plan to be your busiest times? Do you have a product that you think will really sell for Christmas but will be a slow seller that rest of the year? Make sure you plan to spend the majority of your marketing dollars in advance of that season. Plan according to your business's reliance on the seasons for more success.

1. Budget for Your Marketing

I find most entrepreneurs spend an enormous amount of time and money, and focus their budget on the development and manufacturing component, while neglecting the costs associated with marketing.

Marketing your business will be one of your most costly endeavors, so make sure you include this into your budget.

Sharole Lawrence, Marketing Specialist and owner of Glow Marketing, recommends 10 to 15 percent of your budget be allocated to marketing if you are a business-to-business product or service, and 15 to 20 percent of your budget if you are a business-to-consumer product or service. If you know your budget in advance of the upcoming year, you will be less likely to spend in an undisciplined and ineffective way.

Know your objectives when writing your marketing plan. Obviously you want to build revenue, your four-year-old could tell you that — but you also want to build a new customer database, build returning customer business, or multiple streams of revenue from both. Make sure you define these targets and make sure you have the budget and the marketing opportunities to achieve them.

2. Build Your Brand

As your business plan becomes more solidified in your mind and on paper, your brand will need to grow along with it. Hiring a marketing specialist can be out of the price range of a new entrepreneur so make sure you do it correctly yourself from the beginning.

"I like to suggest entrepreneurs begin describing their brand as a person before they start working with a graphic designer. How would they describe them, what personality traits would they have? Once that is done, start looking for pictures that have that same kind of feeling," says Sharole Lawrence. Taking a completed brand plan like this will save you time and money on your graphic design budget because you will have the colors you like, the personality, and the feel laid-out for the graphic designer.

Research must also be included in your marketing plan. Hold small, informal focus groups to find out who your target market is and what they like and dislike about your product. When I began *The MOMpreneur*, we regularly sent out surveys that asked our readers about their favorite articles, topics, and writers. We were always surprised to hear that although they loved the entrepreneurial aspect of the magazine, and that was why they bought it, they appreciated the sex, beauty, and personal relationship articles because it gave them the feel of reading something for fun and for learning as well as communicating with a girlfriend about their personal lives. This was something they wouldn't find in a typical business magazine and it made us stand out, and it made us different.

We also became very clear on who our target market was. They were young, hip mothers with children younger than ten, who had businesses under five years old with fewer than five employees. We knew their yearly revenues, whether they were married, how much they had invested in their businesses, and how they balanced family and work life. It gave us an opening to communicate with them and to build our business as a community.

Know your competition. What are they doing in terms of marketing? How are they communicating to their customers? How are they positioning themselves in the media? Study what they are doing right, what they are doing wrong, and take those lessons and apply them to your plans.

Write a SWOT analysis like the one in Chapter 2. This is a four-part analysis of your strengths, your weaknesses, your opportunities, and your threats that should be done not only on the marketing level but on a larger business-plan scale as well.

Finally, develop a forecast for each marketing initiative that you undertake. Are you planning to do one trade show per year and follow up with a public-relations-focused plan? Fine, but know what you are trying to achieve and measure it. Measure not only your revenue growth and seasonal fluctuations but your website traffic, your social media followers, and your mentions in the media and the virtual world.

3. Tools for Planning Your Marketing Initiatives

Planning your marketing initiatives can be intimidating, especially when you start looking at each individual component's cost. These are a few of the marketing initiatives I have found to be most successful for me as well as some of the most cost-effective.

3.1 Website

Obviously in today's world, you cannot even consider having a business without a website. However, before you build a website, think about what your website will be doing for your business. Is it collecting information for a newsletter, educating your client on your product or service, or positioning you as an expert in your field? Know each of your objectives and plan accordingly.

Websites can be expensive to build. I have tried almost everything to have something that meets my budget and achieves my goals. I have developed my own site from a template, traded services for a website to be developed and maintained, and I have paid almost $25,000 for one to be developed from scratch specifically for my business. Website development has quickly become one of the most complicated and costly expenses in a new start-up.

I like to use TemplateMonster.com. This site has designers from around the globe post website templates. There are thousands to choose from, they include basic sites, e-commerce sites, and flash websites — you name it, they have it. Many of the sites cost less than $100 to purchase, you need only put in your logo and personalized text and it is ready to go. If you don't have the skills to do that yourself, the site can handle it for you, again for the cost of a few hundred dollars. This kind of service can save you thousands and thousands of dollars. Be warned, the downside of this is that others may like the same template you chose and copy it for their businesses. There is the option of buying the site outright so that no one can ever use it, but in my experience, I have never seen any copies of the sites I have purchased and once you add your logo and change the color schemes to match your branding, it becomes unique.

If you have been in business for a few years, or you are just starting your business, you should consider the following:

- ☛ Make sure your website has been submitted to Bing, Yahoo!, and Google for North American markets (search for "submit site" for details on how to do this).

- ☛ Review your site to make sure it clearly states what you do and who you are.

- ☛ Regularly add new content. People want fresh content and things that are relevant today. Supplement content with blogs, postings, and follow up with social media to guide traffic back to your site.

3.2 Search engine optimization

"I paid almost $10,000 to have my website built, but it just wasn't getting the traffic I had hoped. It wasn't until I started adding updates, blogging about the products and services, and posting reviews that I began to see our numbers grow. It certainly didn't happen overnight."

— Rose, Washington, DC

Search engine optimization (SEO) is a term that you should be familiar with and if you are not, you need to become familiar with it. You need to know how quickly your business name comes up and with what ranking when potential clients search key words related to your product or service on the Internet. Your home page should be first when someone types in your business name into a search engine, if it does not, you need to find someone who can fix that immediately.

To optimize your ratings on the top search engines on the Internet, the following are some tips to consider:

- Have a website that defines what you do, what it is you are selling, and who you are selling to. These words, terms, and comments are indexed by search engines. Write for your customers, not for search engines. This may sound basic but many entrepreneurs don't do this. Often the first page is about deals and financing options, but not products or services.

- Submit your website to Google, Bing, and Yahoo! — look on these engines' sites and follow their directions. These tools will start to show you what they think you are about; if this isn't consistent with your ideas — then you need to alter the site to get it to match.

- Regularly update your site and promote it — social media, word of mouth, build an email list, or use pay-per-click ads. Start with Google AdWords to supplement your rankings at the beginning.

- Get a professional SEO consultant to review your title tags, header tags, and overall website. Check the consultant's references.

- You need to measure and analyze your SEO statistics. Some content-management platforms will do this for you (e.g., WordPress). I use Google Analytics for traffic results for my sites.

- Have someone else read your website and tell you what he or she thinks it is about. If someone else can't figure it out, it is not a well-written site.

3.3 Social media

"Social media is the most cost-effective way for us to not only market our products, but to gain feedback on new ideas and designs as well. Social media has become not only the cool thing for companies to do, but the necessary thing. Mommy bloggers have tremendous impact on purchases today; it's absolutely integral for companies to have a social media campaign that reaches out to them."

— Jane Walter, organicKidz

In 1997, 50 million people were using the Internet in the US. Facebook gained more than 100 million users between January 2009 and January 2010. Social media can no longer be ignored, especially as the owner of a new and cash-strapped business. Tools I focus on are Facebook, Twitter, and LinkedIn, all for their own individual benefits.

Facebook is a great opportunity to build a fan page for your site. You can post photos of products, events, awards, and updates to clients, suppliers, and friends. It allows people to comment on your services, see your product, and can almost act as a business's website with applications to sell your product directly from the page.

Twitter is a different kind of communication that takes some getting used to if you are not already on board. You need to learn to communicate in a much more succinct fashion and learn to build conversations and follow others using much less language than ever before. I use services such as HootSuite to manage my social media accounts; search for competition; watch for people that mention me or my services and products; and post and schedule messages about events I am attending, things my clients are doing that would be of interest to others, awards, or links to helpful information. Again, it is so important to know why you are undertaking certain initiatives before investing time and money into managing them.

I work on my social media community to build my reputation as an expert in the community of women in business and more specifically mothers balancing entrepreneurship. I look for women I can partner with, women I can learn from, and women who may be a good match for me as a client. I do not post personal messages about me or my family and I don't post anything I don't think others will be interested in. In fact, I often stop following others who do. I consider them to be wasting my time if they post messages about taking out their garbage or what is on TV. I just don't have the time to sift through that mundane information. I do look for links to new products, new and interesting businesses, and articles I find informative or entertaining.

LinkedIn is a more professional site that allows you to post your résumé, look for other colleagues in your field, and post messages to those colleagues. It is a more professional online community-building service that has no place for what is happening in your personal life from moment to moment. This allows you to update people on your clients, your employment opportunities, your new skill developments, and any new career developments that have arisen.

I think the most important lesson I have learned is that you should listen before you speak. Do not communicate with your followers *only* when you are trying to sell something or launching a new product. Make sure you show your followers that you are committed to a sustainable conversation. Retweet helpful information, make recommendations, and post messages about other interesting events or opportunities — this cannot only be about you.

3.4   Blogs

"I'm not so keen on the word 'blogging'; it conjures an 'online diary' vibe rather than a content-driven platform with which to communicate with existing and prospective clients. But regardless of what we call it, blogging is the largest component (and certainly the root) of my online marketing efforts. As I've gradually moved the business model from in-person design services to consulting, planning, and designing virtually, blogging has allowed me to reveal who I am and how I work, not to mention showcase my portfolio quickly and easily as projects evolve and finish. Just like I hop online to research and plan before a major purchase, my clients are looking to build a sense of confidence in how I work, and most importantly, in me, before even thinking of hitting the 'contact' button. For this reason, a blog is essential. Besides, my clients are a savvy bunch; they inspire me to step it up and bring it in a way that a static site never could."

— Erica Swanson, Erica Swanson Design

Blogs can be another opportunity to build your reputation as an expert in your field as well as give you more content to build Google or other search-engine rankings. It also offers you content to discuss in your social media campaigns.

Make sure you follow proper online blog etiquette; for example, don't continuously pitch your product for people to buy. Try to balance your online communication with 10 percent promotion of your product or service and 90 percent information and entertainment supporting your product or service.

I regularly write for blogs across North America. I write about women in business and the challenges they face and how they have overcome them. I end my articles with a short 20-word bio on where to find out more about me and how to find me on Twitter, LinkedIn, and Facebook. People begin to watch for my articles and content because they know that they will not get a continuous sales push and because I focus my content to my target market. They will read my articles because they know they will learn something helpful. The most common and free software for blogging is WordPress but there are many others to choose from.

3.5 Celebrity gifting suites

One of my current businesses, Wild Octopus Inc., represents manufacturers of juvenile and baby products across North America to boutiques and mass-market stores. One of our main marketing initiatives is attending Hollywood gifting suites. These events invite celebrities that have recently had babies and allow businesses to give samples to each of the celebrities and have their photos taken with each celebrity in attendance. The media attendance is high so the chance of having your product shown with a celebrity in magazines that feature celebrity gossip is high. This is a different kind of marketing but drives your product into the realm of a "must have" for people who follow this kind of news.

A master of this kind of initiative is Jane Walter, owner of organicKidz stainless steel baby bottles. Within the course of her first year of production, her bottles had appeared in *US Weekly* with "Octomom," and had been in the hands of Charlie Sheen, Sarah Jessica Parker, and Matthew McConaughey. Make sure you post these events, press appearances, and celebrity endorsements on your site.

3.6 Trade shows

Trade shows may seem like an antiquated and costly initiative for your marketing campaign, but continue to be one of the most important opportunities of the year if you choose them correctly. Make sure you know why you are using this marketing venue. Are you looking to sell your product to businesses, consumers, build some buzz around your business, and build your social media and newsletter followings?

Have a goal and make sure you plan accordingly. Your goal of attending a trade show needs to be more multifaceted than just to close sales; you need to network with your colleagues, meet suppliers and potential customers, and build your online following.

Don't rely on trade show organizers as your only source to drive traffic, make sure you have taken equal accountability in making this a good show for your business. If the trade show is in a different region than where you normally work, invite guests from your database. This gives you an opportunity to solidify relationships.

Roughly 70 percent of trade show attendees know who they are going to visit before ever getting to the show. Do your best to book appointments to meet with them while they are there. Give them some special attention as opposed to hoping they will remember to come and maybe being away from the booth when they arrive. You can also consider requesting the trade show organizer to send you a list of confirmed attendees so that you can target who you want to meet and when and how you will do so. Most professional shows now offer this courtesy.

Before going into a trade show, be aware of the rules of trade show etiquette. Most exhibitors do not like other exhibitors entering their booths — even just to network; make sure you are not stepping on anyone's toes in an effort to build your community.

To get more exposure, consider offering to the show organizers your services as a speaker or to sit in on a panel discussion or participate in judging a contest for an audience. You can also see what media has been invited and should make sure you have sent them your press kit, or have your media package with you so that your product or service stands out from the crowd.

3.7 YouTube

What was once an opportunity to post videos of your kid's first birthday or your teenager's stupid tricks for family members around the globe, YouTube has quickly become an opportunity for the small business to demonstrate the usefulness of its product or service, how to use the product or service, and to show marketing material that is complimentary to its business.

As your business grows, consider posting media interviews and special events to YouTube and linking these back to your site, as well as instructional information or instructions on how to care for your product. These are quick and easy additions to a website and add an extra level of content that will allow you to stand out from the crowd.

Here are some videos that I think are fantastic models:

- ☙ http://www.youtube.com/watch?v=KmIxwwXUFRM
- ☙ http://www.youtube.com/watch?v=2UKbRr3TSu0

3.8 Podcasts

Podcasts are like a taped radio show or audio file that is easily posted to your site. Similar to videos on YouTube, podcasts offer a different kind of learning opportunity for your customers and allows them to get to know you and your business' personality better. The software I use is AudioAcrobat because I can tape over the phone or interview others over the phone and it is automatically saved and filed as an audio file ready to link to my site within four hours. (Note that there are many different providers of this service to choose from.) The cost is also minimal, usually about $20 per month.

Podcasts are an especially important tool for those trying to establish themselves as an expert on a particular topic; it adds another level of content you can publish for your potential clients. For those who become especially adept at this, look into posting your free podcast to iTunes for even more exposure. It is easy and cost effective to do so.

One of my businesses uses podcasts to regularly feature its products and interview the manufacturers of the products. It increases understanding of the products and increases sales because of that understanding. Go to www.wildoctopus.ca/scwibble for a sample.

3.9 Email marketing

"To date, no matter what marketing initiative I try, email marketing continues to be my most profitable."

— Joanne, San Antonio, Texas

Email marketing has got to be one of the largest drivers in sales in all of my businesses to date. From the conception of each business, my goal has been to collect the email addresses of potential clients and people within my target market. I can collect emails through a gift basket giveaway contest at a trade show or by giving away a free gift, such as an e-book for customers that sign up for my newsletter.

I use services such as MyMailout.com or ConstantContact.com to support the newsletters and make sure they don't go directly into someone's spam or junk mail box.

I also regularly subscribe to online newsletters. I subscribe to my competitors newsletters, my potential clients, as well as topics I am just generally interested in. To sign up for the newsletter for this book, go to www.entrepreneurialmombook.com.

3.10 Online reviews

More consumers are turning to online reviews to make a decision before making a purchase. If you have developed a product, make sure you consider sending product samples to influential online reviewers to help build some buzz around your product. However, there is the risk of getting a bad review. If you look at it as positive feedback, you can usually respond to the reviewer and comment on how you will fix the issue or what the reviewer can do to avoid any problems. Most reviewers are easy to find with a quick search on the Internet.

3.11 Awards

"Going after awards was an integral part of our marketing plan. It allowed us a new press release each time we won and we gained tremendous exposure from some of the award companies, which is how we became DisneyFamily.com's Top Green and Organic Product. Our awards are always the focal point around our booth layout at all trade shows. This has helped build our brand as the safer, greener baby bottle."

— Jane Walter, organicKidz

As the popularity for awards grows among entrepreneurs in every industry, more and more award opportunities have become available to small-business entrepreneurs.

Not all awards are free to enter so you need to make sure that you are not wasting your time or money applying for an award that is not going to be a marketing opportunity. For the awards you need to pay for (e.g., Parent Tested Parent Approved Award or the Juvenile Products Manufacturers Association Innovation awards), make sure they are well worth the nominal fee, especially if you win.

Award winners benefit from having coverage on the Web, attention at events, and a press release that often garners media attention. Make sure you find award programs suited to your industry and always make sure you understand the rules before entering.

3.12 In-person networking

Now I know you are all going to roll your eyes when you read that I want you to continue to show up to those networking events with their "rubber chicken dinners" and barrages of sales pitches. It is important to maintain a face-to-face relationship with people, even if you cannot see how they could help you now or in the future. You never know who will recommend you or mention you to others in the virtual world or media community, or just as another word-of-mouth referral.

Networking events were my main source of marketing when I began *The MOMpreneur Magazine*; the events I attended were specifically geared to my market and led me to the majority of my client relationships in the first few years. To this day, I enjoy attending events just to follow up on the friends I have made and to stay in touch. Even if I am not looking for sales directly, it may be an opportunity to network or to help another woman who is just getting started in business.

3.12a Seven steps to successful networking

Any entrepreneur knows that being a business owner is more about sales than anything else, whether you are in hot tar roofing, algae scraping, or pooper-scooping. It doesn't matter what you do, you must be a salesperson to make a business work. One method that has continually proven successful for many businesses, including mine, is regular networking.

Now I know what you all are thinking, "If I have to eat one more rubber chicken dinner with a bunch of people that I will never hear from again, I am going to poke my eyes out with a spoon." Fear not, I have the magic steps to make networking one of your most successful investments.

The rubber chicken isn't the best bang for your $50, but it isn't the grub you're after, is it? You want to see that cash in your pockets at the end of the month. You want to build your current client relationships and make new ones while they are all in one room, not by making 50 different cold calls to 50 different offices. So get your Imodium and your business cards ready!

Here are seven steps to make networking work for you:

1. "Sign up for at least two different networking groups and go consistently," says Jo-Ann Vacing, Director of the Calgary Chapter of E-Women Networking Group. "It will expand your contact base tremendously."

2. Go with a goal of making contacts, not sales. Sales will not happen in your first visit and maybe not your second; you need to slowly build relationships on trust and a foundation of consistent appearances. People want to know they are not dealing with a fly-by-night business.

3. Hone your message and make it sexy and *short*! If I have to hear one more message that uses "cutting edge," "one of a kind," or "groundbreaking," I am going to barf. Kim Duke, The Sales Diva Inc., calls this "info dumping," and don't worry, we all catch ourselves doing it. Just learn to recognize that glazed over, "I would rather have a colonoscopy than talk to you" look and cut it off!

4. Go with your gear. There is nothing worse that meeting a contact with whom you would like to follow up, and she doesn't have a business card or she asks to write on the back of yours! This is an extremely tacky move.

5. Learn how to listen. People want to be asked about themselves, so make listening and asking questions your priority in these meetings. Make them enjoy their time with you rather than making them desperate for an escape route.

6. Stand out! This is the time to pull out your best red shoes and your most fabulous peacock blue shirt — I don't care what you do, just stand out (but keep it classy)!

7. Follow up. If you are not going to take the time to follow up with the connections you have made, then you might as well not even go. This is the most crucial step in making this marketing component work. Even if a sale never comes from that person, you never know who she might connect you with in the future.

The next time you are thinking that you need to pump up your bottom line, think about investing some time and money into the right networking group for you. It may take some time to find the right one but it will definitely be worth the wait, just don't forget to take an antacid with you. You just might need it.

4. Building Your Own Public Relations Campaign

Public Relations (PR) was the focus of the marketing campaign for *The MOMpreneur Magazine*. Not only did it build national awareness of the website and the magazine, but it built my reputation as an expert on balancing motherhood and being an entrepreneur. Our media campaign was successful because we planned it with the following objectives:

- I chose three key marketing messages and I knew them by heart. I could recite them clearly, concisely, and could bring a conversation back to them if the interview was heading away from my objectives.

- We started small, approaching local media in my city. This allowed me to build a strong support base in my local community and it saved me a tremendous amount on travel expenses.

- I included influential women bloggers and website owners as a part of my media campaign. Traditional media was fantastic for building our public awareness; online press coverage solidified our growing online subscribers. We were targeting women who spent time reading on the Internet because that was what we wanted them to do on our site. Coverage on sites such as Savvymom.ca and YummyMummyClub.ca were invaluable and often increased our online subscriptions by thousands on the days the articles ran.

- We sent out lots of samples of the magazines. Don't expect people to write about you without experiencing your product. One of my biggest pet peeves at *The MOMpreneur Magazine* was having people request a product mention or review but not send a sample because it was too costly. They wanted free publicity but would not send a sample! I considered it extremely rude and opportunistic. Besides, how could I have promoted a product I knew nothing about or was not able to test? I would never have made the mistake of endorsing something that could have turned out to be bad for my market. When you approach the media, keep this in mind and consider the cost of the sample against the value of the publicity from the media mention or review. Get to know journalists. Find them through sites such as Mastheads.org and EasyMediaList.com. Know what their interests are, what they write about, and what topics they are looking for. Follow them on Twitter and Facebook. If you know they are looking for a story that has nothing to do with you but would work well for a colleague, recommend the person if for nothing else than to build a relationship with that journalist. The journalist will remember you the next time a story comes up where it might be a good opportunity for you to be mentioned.

- Don't follow the "spray and pray" model of sending out press releases. Send the release only to journalists that write about similar topics, products, and services. Target where you want that release to go, where you want publicity to appear, and how you will use it to go forward.

- Be current. Watch the news and read the paper and online websites daily. Follow media on Twitter if you don't have time to watch or read the entire piece. If a story is active and can somehow relate to you or you can comment, send in a press release. Always be prepared to make a statement to the media or to appear live.

- Follow up if you haven't heard back about a press release. As the owner of a niche magazine, we often received more than 100 press releases per day. It is hard to keep track, so make sure you follow up with an email or phone call to make sure it was read and that the reader understood the content.

- Say thank you. If you get some publicity, please make sure to say thank you. Journalists notice this and it gives them another opportunity to remember you.

Media campaigns have become so important to today's marketing plans that I recently decided to invest in the growth of one myself. Building Alchemy Communications Inc. (www.alchemycommunications.ca) not only allows me to focus on building the reputations of other entrepreneurial women within the community of women viewing the media, but it also allows me to stay current with media trends. Hiring a professional to secure quality interviews for your campaign can be worth the minimal amount of monetary investment.

If your goal is to get on the Oprah Network or Rachael Ray, don't plan on that happening with a homemade do-it-yourself press release. Securing one of those outlets can be the tipping point for your company to become the next big thing. If an opportunity is worth $100,000 in potential revenue, then budget and plan for a professional to handle the public relations for you. For sample media kits, press pages, and press releases, go to www.entrepreneurialmombook.com.

Sample 4 is a template for a press release.

4.1 Media kit

A media kit gives the reader all of the information he or she needs to pull a story together including the following:

Sample 4
PRESS RELEASE

Headline

Summary Paragraph – a quick review of the story, main details

City, State, Month 1, 2011 – The first paragraph is known as the "lede." It contains the most important information. You need to grab your readers' attention here. You can't assume that they have read the headline or summary paragraph; the lede needs to be able to give the reader enough information to stand alone.

Body: The body of the press release needs to include who, what, where, when, and why components in short, succinct sentences similar to a news story.

For extra attention, you may want to include a quote by the main person in the story or someone close to the story.

The last paragraph needs to summarize the key points of the press release.

Company Summary: include pertinent details of the company in a short paragraph.

Contact Information:

Your Name
Title
Company Name
Phone Number
you@youremailaddress.com
Yourwebsite.com

- High-resolution images of person or product
- Press release
- Supplementary information (i.e., company history)
- Prior media coverage
- Details of product, if applicable

This information can be sent in the mail in a folder, but most outlets now prefer digital files to be emailed or downloaded from website press pages.

4.2 Press pages

If media coverage is going to be a mainstay within your marketing plan, be sure to include a press page for easy media access. On this page, include:

- Downloadable high-resolution images
- Press releases (current and archived)
- Company history
- Product details
- All prior coverage

Case Study: Disney's Marketing

As soon as you become a mom and start envisioning the first family vacation, most women start to envision the Magic Kingdom and their children being swept away with the fairy tales and fun of DisneyWorld. I was no different. Last month, we finally got the opportunity. Four days of relaxation; a commitment to leave the smartphones and laptops at home and connect to the magic of my kid's first vacation with Mickey Mouse. Terrifying, I know.

My intention was not to work one iota, and I tried, I really did, but being a small-business consultant, as well as the founder of an entrepreneurial magazine and website, I couldn't help but notice the perfection of the Disney business model. I decided to do a case study on the happiest place on earth and bring it back to my network of entrepreneurial moms.

Many of you may think the model of Disney is way out of your league, but what I found was quite the opposite; Disney has chosen to implement many different tools of success from which many of us could learn. The following are a few that I thought you might like.

Multiple streams of revenue

I know many of you are a bit jaded when discussing the amount of shopping opportunities at Disney, but from an entrepreneurial perspective, we can all learn something. Obviously Disney's streams of revenue focus on the park tickets, the accommodations, and the souvenirs, but if you look closely, there are opportunities to purchase items and services so that you can stay longer at the park. For example, they offer strollers, baby-care centers including beautiful nursing stations, and quiet areas to rest, relax, and refresh before forging ahead on the next adventure. They sell raincoats, rain boots, socks, sweaters, coats: everything so that your magical moments are not disrupted by inclement weather. A girlfriend mentioned, "I didn't care if that stroller cost $100 per day, I would have spent it to stay longer at the park." (Actual cost is $15 per day.) I can't say that this didn't make me spend a lot of time thinking about streams of revenue I could add that would make it easier for my clients to purchase from me.

Customer service

I don't know of any other corporation who handles customer service better than Disney. From the moment you arrive on the grounds to the moment you leave, you and every member of your family is treated like royalty. You don't realize how uncommon this is until you can see a contrast. I have to admit, it fascinated me and I began to test them. I watched every person from the housekeeping staff to their national directory of media relations with my family and with other guests at the parks — it never changed.

I had the opportunity to speak to a stroller rental attendant during a particularly complex diaper change that my husband was handling and had to start asking questions. Her reply was fascinating. She told me that when she started, she was trained for about five minutes on the cash register and from that moment on, her professional development has been focused on making every moment "magical" for every guest in the park that she comes in contact with. She told me that Disney had done research on what adults remember most of their childhood Disney experience and it was usually one employee of the corporation making a moment magical. I began to think of my recent communications with clients and although I feel I try to be attentive to their needs, I am not sure I can say that the moments I create are that memorable, at least not consistently.

Disney's moments are not created with large investments of time or money. It can take only a sticker, addressing the girls as "princess" or the boys as "mouseketeer," or having the life-sized Tigger pose with a favorite bear rather than hug a skittish child whose mother talks too much about "stranger danger." Watching these moments was fascinating and made such a difference to our trip. Disney has become so good at this that they are now offering the Disney Institute for corporations to come and learn about the Disney models of customer service. If you are interested in attending one in person or virtually, go to Disney Institute online. (Another interesting stream of revenue: delivering information virtually and in person.)

Website marketing

Next time you are thinking of planning a vacation or just hanging out with your kids on the computer, visit Disney.com (there is also a Disney.ca site that provides Canadian travel specials), and see how you can duplicate some of their ideas to keep people on your site longer. I could spend hours on the site reading mommy blogs, looking at vacation planners, or playing video games that are for every age group. Disney's ability to capitalize on online marketing is like no other. You cannot get better top-of-mind awareness than when your four-year-old asks hourly to play the new *Alice in Wonderland* game.

Consider how interesting your site is, and whether it encourages your clients to stick around and return on a daily basis. What could be added so that it would create repeat visitors? Are you taking advantage of social media sites that are free of charge and that encourage top-of-mind awareness?

Media and public relations

I have to admit, it would be hard for a small-business owner to compete with Disney in sending a group of media for a one-week vacation at your place of business, but what we can learn from is the pieces that made me as a media member want to write about that business. Disney has been around since 1955; you have to admit, it is hard to continue to write press releases each year — the media and the public needs a new story.

Recently Disney launched "Give a Day, Get a Disney Day," which is a volunteer campaign. This was an initiative that gave one free Disney park pass in return for one day of volunteering at select registered charities. It encouraged families to volunteer and give back to their communities together while encouraging travel to the park.

This is brilliant in terms of a campaign to drive traffic to the parks as well as the media attention it garnered. It is also something most businesses can do in their own special way. Find a charity in your area that relates to your target market and find a way to partner with it so that you both benefit. The leverage this kind of campaign could potentially have makes it a marketing model we should all look at.

The press event was also very interesting. I always look to see where I am seated in relation to where others are to see my hierarchy in the Canadian media. Disney did something very interesting this time: Ahead of all of the Canadian media was a much larger section called "Social Media Moms." This was a group you know I was going to be spending some time with. What I found fascinating was that these were not large business websites backed by big corporations, these were moms at home whose blogs have attracted a lot of attention and traffic, and Disney knew their influence was integral to reaching its target market. How much time have you spent blogging, and if your business is something in the juvenile/mom arena, have you addressed this component of new media? Take a look at YoYoMama.ca and LiteraryMama.com for some great bloggers you should know.

I could go on and on about how much I loved spending time at DisneyWorld, learning about making my businesses better, and I would encourage you to start to look at bigger players like Disney when writing your marketing plans or even business plans. Not only was DisneyWorld a once-in-a-lifetime family vacation that we will never forget, but I feel like I came back reinvigorated and ready to be more creative with my new business initiatives based on what I saw. Sometimes, we don't need to reinvent the wheel, only add our personal or, dare I say, "magical" touch.

9

Preparing a Sales Plan

Sales are challenging, and unless you were born to be a salesperson, you will feel the stress of each deal from start to finish. If you are like me, sales come easily; if not, and you feel your bowels turn to ice water at the thought of cold calling, then you need to work harder to solidify your sales plan and build a sales team of people who enjoy the rush of closing a deal.

1. Forecasting Sales

Forecasting or predicting your sales for the next year or upcoming years is a challenge, especially if your business is new or math is not your forte. Once you have a strong handle on your expenses you should be able to take them to a bookkeeper to help you analyze your cash flow. See www.entrepreneurialmombook.com for a template and directions.

At the beginning of each year, the biggest tip I can give you is to gear up your sales team so that they want to go out and take the market share from your competitors. To do this, you will need clear targets and goals, broken down by month, to which you or your team will be held accountable.

In times of recession, planning becomes even more challenging. If you find your targets are drastically off from what you have predicted, you may need to evaluate your targets monthly versus yearly, until the market evens out. The most important piece is to measure your sales, review them monthly against your targets, and evaluate whether you can do better or your team can achieve more and how. Maybe it is engaging in a new social-media campaign, increasing cold calls, or attending more networking events — whatever it is, keep your goals in focus.

To help you develop your sales plan, I contacted Kim Duke (international sales expert, owner of The Sales Divas, and one of my sales mentors) to give you a leg up on your competition. Here is a transcript of my interview with her:

How would you recommend to an entrepreneurial mom develop a sales plan?

One of the first words that popped into my mind was "carefully." Too many entrepreneurs jump into the world of owning their own business with absolutely *no plan* for how they are going to attract clients.

Developing a sales plan requires research. Winging it does not work here! You need to know your market — is there a demand for your product? How many competitors do you have and what are their rates? How long is your anticipated sales cycle? (The more expensive the product — the longer the sales cycle can be.) Yearly, quarterly, monthly, and weekly sales targets are essential to also stay on track.

Of course, you also need a list of qualified prospects and what the expected sales would be.

Remember: Not doing a sales plan is *not* an option.

What is the biggest mistake women make in sales?

Mistake number 1: Women mistake closing a sale as some intrusive, icky, nasty thing they have to do. Forget about the phrase "closing the sale" and instead think "opening the door for business."

Mistake number 2: Women don't ask enough questions throughout the sales process which means they don't know if they're the best fit for the client.

Mistake number 3: Women typically give too much away for free, hoping that it will convince the potential customer to buy from them. (It won't.)

What is the best way women can ensure a successful sales plan?

One of the biggest factors harming you is that not enough people know about you and what you provide. You need to create a presence and a brand by networking with the proper channels, creating strategic alliances, using Facebook, Twitter, etc. in a proper manner (talking about your dog constantly does *not* create business), asking for referrals, and making damn sure that you know *why* you're different and *why* a customer should buy from you. If you don't know this, how is a customer supposed to know?

You need to clearly know your niche, what you offer that is unique to the marketplace, and the demand for your service. Do not pick a team of people who are all like you. You need diversity of personalities and selling styles, but everyone has to have the same work ethic and goal.

As the owner of a growing business, it is not always feasible to be doing 100 percent of the sales yourself, even though you are probably the best at selling your product or service. What is the best way to establish a sales team to sell your product?

You can certainly delegate your sales as long as you are willing to pay for it and monitor it closely. Most entrepreneurs want "someone else to do that nasty sales stuff" and they either pay too much for little results or they expect someone to bust their butt for 100 percent commission (even though it takes time to establish sales relationships). You will need to spend money to make money in this case. But stay on top of it and make sure you've picked the right person or people for the job.

Leading a team requires just that: leading. You can't be everyone's friend. Your role is to inspire, support, and provide all the tools necessary for your team's success. Sometimes that means you have to say "no." Sometimes it means you're going to have to go on sales calls. One of the worst things you can do is to micromanage the team and then expect superior results.

Focus on creating a community of people who are prospects, clients, and suppliers. Understand that referrals are one of the fastest ways you can grow your business and that you *have to ask for them*.

If you'd like more free, sassy, and savvy sales advice, I'd suggest heading to www.salesdivas.com. (How's that for shameless self-promotion?)

2. Cold Calling

I have to admit, I am not a fan of cold calling, although, I have paid my dues and figured out I needed to have some kind of brand recognition before it would work. For me, the shift away from cold calling happened when I started to build a more public profile for myself. Between writing articles, doing media, and speaking at networking groups, my profile as an expert in the field of entrepreneurial moms grew. As this profile grew, more people wanted to work with me. As soon as I took my focus from contacting people about making a sale, to building my profile as an expert and someone who had valued clients that offered referrals, my sales started coming. Now, I don't have to solicit sales at all, I only act on referrals.

To build on your profile as an expert in your community, rely on your marketing plan to drive your opportunity to get in front of your community. Write articles, write a blog, use email marketing, network, and send out media pitches, but stop focusing on begging for sales.

3. Terms of Sale

Part of being a successful entrepreneur is having strong boundaries in place. Too many women give away too much for too little because they are afraid of a rejection or low sales. I find if you have established rules and boundaries, people respect you because of it and want to buy from you because you have moved past the mistakes of a typical microbusiness in its early years. Some of the guidelines you need to have in place are your terms of sale.

4. Credit Policy

It doesn't take a brain surgeon to figure out if you have a client with $10,000 cash and $15,000 credit, that you have an opportunity to make a $25,000 sale. Offering credit to your clients can be both lucrative and risky. With this offering, you need to plan on having some debts go bad, but it may be worth it in the end. Here is where your cash flow and risk tolerance come in handy. Make sure you have a strong understanding of both.

There are two kinds of credit you can look into: open credit and revolving credit. Open credit usually entails submitting an invoice and offering "net 30" or giving your client 30 days to pay. Revolving credit is more along the lines of a credit card, where you give your client $15,000 credit based on approval, and the client pays chunks or the full amount on the outstanding balance.

I like to offer terms of sale that include a discount for early payments. I will often offer a 2 to 5 percent discount on an invoice if it is paid within 10 days. I also demand a penalty in the initial agreement if payment is late or past 30 days at 2 to 5 percent per annum. You need to get this in writing before you begin to offer your product or service, and make sure you include a deferral of your legal costs to the client if you need to collect.

Managing Your Relationships

As your business grows, it is fairly safe to say that your free time will shrink. Add in a splash of mommy guilt for the overtime hours and a spouse feeling neglected, and you get a perfect storm. Keeping your personal relationships in balance will be a skill that you will continuously need to build because I guarantee you, if your personal life is falling apart (e.g., your family is unhappy), you have lost sight of why you went down the road to being an entrepreneurial mom.

1. Remember Your Spouse's Place in Your Life

"I worked with my partner for two years. It was good, there were challenges; however, there were boundaries set and followed by both of us to ensure the best outcome possible. It was a well-executed plan prior to initialization. We needed to have a clear definition of what our roles were both in our employment positions as well as personal relationship positions. Communication was the key to our success. There were also very stressful moments, as both of us were working for the same company; our financial well-being was dependent on the same source. If I could choose to do it all again, I would choose to do things differently.

I believe financial stress is harder on couples than anything else, especially when you are supporting children."

— Jessica Jacobs, Little Soles Inc.

Being the spouse or life partner of an entrepreneurial mother is not for the faint of heart. The men I have met and interviewed, including my own husband, have a tremendous amount of guts and self-confidence to be married to someone with a big, ambitious personality.

I have been blessed by being married to a wonderful man, fantastic father and, above all, my number one fan. When everyone else was gone, he was there. When there was not a penny left, he was still there. Despite his ongoing support, the only thing we fight about is money.

Having chosen to be an entrepreneur, I have chosen a life of fluctuating income, that is largely reliant on an economy that fluctuates as well. Although I have passed the time in my career where I take risks that are high, especially since I have had children, there is still the potential of losing my investment of time and money on a project that goes south.

In the most difficult times of even my most successful projects, I have gone months without a paycheck, overused a personal credit card, and stressed my marriage in order to keep the business alive. Am I proud to admit this? No. Have I learned from it? Yes.

In one particularly heated fight, my husband was angry that I had used our money to pay yet another business expense. He felt I had other options, including making my investors step up to the plate. He said that he felt that I was choosing the business over the financial stability of our family. He was right. I shouldn't have spent any more of our money on a business that would need much more than I could provide. It was a hard pill to swallow, but I had to acknowledge that I had come to the end of my time with that company. I had to move on to make room for someone else with deeper pockets, or lose majority rights with the company — something that I wasn't willing to do. In order to move forward from that conflict, I had to choose my family first and focus on projects that had larger and more secure streams of income.

Looking back, there were things I could have done much differently. Going forward, I now have the financial ability and connections to finance a business outside of of using my own funds. If I had to do it again, I would include my husband in the initial business planning. I would have known earlier what point would cause too much stress for him and what he needed from me in order to feel comfortable with the growth of the company. Luckily, we were able to make changes quickly enough to preserve our marriage and our friendship. I look back and realize how risky it was to ignore his stress over the situation. No business is worth losing my marriage.

From a professional perspective, Janet Miller, psychologist, advises:

❦ If you're in business for yourself, then it's a known fact that you're going to go through some hard times — psychologically, financially, and logistically — you'll be busy, at times you'll be preoccupied, and likely at some point you'll feel very financially stressed. If you can, talk with your partner before the crisis occurs. Have a "what if" conversation, and work together to figure out your individual and collective values, tolerance for risk, need/desire to "be in the know," and decision-making style before you're put to the test. If you can, work out some boundaries. Maybe try including some early warning indicators that will signal that it's time to talk; for example:

- "Honey, this is my dream and I am really excited to be opening my own business. That being said, I know that there is a financial risk here — and we're married; I love you, and I know that you love me. I'm wondering if we can talk about some of those risks now just so I can have a sense of how you see things. Would that be okay?"

- "Let's say that we need to invest some [or some more] of our own money into this business of mine. How much would be too much for you? At what point would you want to say, 'no more'? [Let's say your partner says $50,000.] Okay, so can we agree that if our personal debt reaches the $30,000 mark, we can book some time to sit down together and talk about the situation? [Early warning sign.]"

❦ Checking in with your spouse often. Really listening to what he or she is saying is strongly recommended. Remember, this person likely does want your business to succeed more than anyone else, but likely he or she also wants you to be relaxed, confident, relatively stress-free, and financially stable. When your spouse gives you a hard time, do what you can to listen for the love behind the words or behind the tone.

Blog Post: Working with Husband (February 2010)

One of the common threads of the emails I have received is how to deal with that troublesome husband; you know, the one who keeps asking you to get a "real" job. Like waking up with the kids at 5:00 a.m., feeding the kids, driving the kids, picking up the kids, feeding the kids, running a business, getting supper ready, bathing the kids, and putting those kids to sleep isn't really work.

I have to admit, my being entrepreneurial has been an issue with my fella. Don't get me wrong, he is a great guy, a great dad, a reliable breadwinner, and, for the most part, will do back flips to keep our family happy. He is also a huge fan of my businesses. When it comes to risk taking, especially financially, I sometimes think he would prefer someone more stable.

Not that he doesn't have reason. Eight weeks into our marriage, I lost a million-dollar-a-year business, mainly due to some bad decisions and being young and immature. It was a crushing blow to me financially and emotionally, I didn't get out of bed for four months. For him, I think it was an experience he would rather not be a part of again, which is understandable.

I remember distinctly one morning he said, "I know! You could get a job as a bus driver!" Like he was possessed by the brilliance of Einstein! He had cured my dilemma; what I would do next to bring some income in on the side! To this day, when I think of that moment, I look for the nearest steel-toed boot to throw. I was incensed! I had built a business with more than 50 staff, and more than $100,000 a month in revenue, and he wanted me to sign up for the nearest entry-level position. Yes, my business crashed and burned but I had built it and grown it over five years. I admit it, out of spite, when I heard him say "become a bus driver," I wrote a business plan to start a national magazine — a touch on the risky side. There was probably some spite involved in making it successful as well. A bit of the old, "I'll show him"!

It isn't easy being married, especially from the entrepreneurial/financial end of things. You want to follow your dreams; he wants a savings account. You want to change the world; he wants to take a vacation this year.

For us, it has come down to some really intense "discussions" over the years. (I say discussion in the broadest sense of the word.) He has said that it feels like I sometimes choose paying those involved in the business (e.g., staff, vendors) before our family, which is not easy to hear. He is right; there have been times when I have chosen to go without so that the business could continue to thrive. I explain that those people need to be paid first so that I can soon be paid — he wants it now. He has a biweekly paying position, why should I not have to get one also? Is it reasonable for me to postpone my love of risk for more stability as our family grows? To this day, I am not sure what the right answer is.

When times are good, he is my biggest supporter; when times are tough, he holds my hand. At all times, he counts the money — I think it is part of his job. I thank him for it 99.9 percent of the time. The other 0.01 percent of the time, I would like to stuff him in the oven and spray him with barbecue sauce!

Here are some tips I've found help me:

- I share my revenue goals for the year with my husband and the expenses I need to have in order to achieve those goals. He says having that information makes him much more comfortable.

- I remind him that I am saving money on childcare because I do not have to go to a "real job" and my earning potential is larger as an entrepreneur.

- I commit to bringing in a certain amount of money each month. If I miss that target, we reassess the plan going forward. Maybe it means taking on another client, working extra hours, or doing some work that I would prefer not to do just to make ends meet.

For me, being entrepreneurial is who I am; making it work for our financial stability is my commitment going forward.

2. Keeping Things Good between You and Your Business Partner

"Jana and I had begun our online business and over the course of two years, had built a strong following of more than 20,000 subscribers. We both had invested $30,000 into growing the business and endless hours of work. Around the two-and-a-half year mark, her husband was offered a really great job in a different state. She let me know she was moving in one month, she was leaving the company, and she wanted me to buy her out within the month. I was shocked, and I felt so betrayed. I wrote her a check, I just couldn't face the hurt of confronting and challenging her on it; she was my best friend."

— Katie, Chicago, Illinois

Working with a business partner can be challenging, especially around communicating and resolving disputes. This person will become a key member in your life and challenges and successes in the business will forge a friendship that (good or bad) will be integral to your success.

Communicating during a dispute and coming to a resolution can be almost as challenging as resolving issues with your spouse. Although it has been said that "we are here to make money, not be friends," your day-to-day operations will be much more enjoyable if you can find a way to work together and strive toward common goals. Dr. Janet Miller, psychologist, advises:

- ♥ Take time to develop that relationship. Work through things that irritate you or push your buttons. Check out your assumptions, listen to one another, get to know each other, and stay connected to your shared vision, your ability to inspire one another, and work towards a common vision.

- ♥ Before there are issues, try to define your roles or scope of practice. Communication is the key. Talk about how you'll deal with disagreements before they occur. For example, you may decide that you'll each consult on major decisions, but when it's in your area, you get to take the lead and have the final say.

- ♥ You may decide to take turns making decisions, or you may decide to "balance things out." For example, "You got to hire two salespeople last month, so now I'm taking the lead on hiring our coordinator."

- ♥ If you're at an impasse on a major decision and your communication gets heated, it might help to go through a logical, sequential "pros and cons" exercise. For example, write down pros and cons for each idea. Consider the good and the bad of going with each idea, and also what might be gained or lost by not going with the idea. Then highlight the pieces that fit with your company's vision. Attempt this exercise individually, and then come together to discuss your results. You might discover that this exercise is enough to shift your points of view.

❦ Take the time to develop a "decision-making rubric," which is something that will guide your decision-making process in this business. What are your goals? What values are most important to you? How does this issue fit in with your goal or vision? How will the decision impact your company and its vision or goals? Will it keep you on track?

- For example, if your goal is to break even the first year, then this isn't the time to load up on supplies that will last you five years. If your goal is to expand, then perhaps you'll be hiring more people. If your goal is to support innovative ideas, then you'll be taking bigger risks. If your goal is to value your long-time customers, then you will be building relationships. If your goal is to increase visibility, then you'll be spending more time and money on marketing. If your goal is to be an eco-friendly company, then you might agree to spend more on products because of their ethical development. Your common vision will help to guide your decision-making process, and referencing how your decisions fit with your company's vision will help.

❦ If you're having a hard time hearing one another and it really is a major decision, then consider discussing the issue with an impartial (but informed) third party. Consultation can be very helpful.

❦ Sleep on it. If possible, don't make large, contentious decisions in the heat of the moment.

❦ Your biggest critic is often a great ally. Having a partner that challenges you to see things differently can be really stimulating and can help you to form better decisions in the end. Spend time getting to know one another personally, not just professionally — this might help you to understand why some issues are really important to your partner, while others are not.

❦ If you're having a hard time "letting go" of an idea or perspective, try to take some time to reflect on why this particular issue is so intense for you. Sometimes here-and-now problems bring up older issues — times we felt unheard, stepped on, disrespected, or had our point of view discounted. It could be that this issue really isn't as "hot" as we thought it was — it just reminds us of past stuff that we might wish to deal with and put to rest. If this is the case, take it as a gift — self-awareness cannot be underrated!

Take the time to negotiate early on how you will resolve a dispute, otherwise you will have to pay lawyers and judges to decide for you.

3. Customer Relations

One of the reasons I experienced some success with *The MOMpreneur Magazine* was the fact that we strived for really great customer service. Although it wasn't easy keeping up with the entrepreneurial moms, I tried to keep tabs on who was doing what, and what was going on in their family lives, and their businesses — I tried to connect regularly if they had shown any interest in becoming a customer. This not only built relationships and sales in the company, but many friendships as well. Adding staff on to take this task over, needed someone just as dedicated to getting to know these women, understanding their marketing plans, and knowing what was going on in their lives. My clientele were entrepreneurial moms, which meant I needed to know about their kids, their lives, and how they balanced work and family — at least enough to have a good conversation with them when we met at a networking event or online.

Building customer service takes time, it takes committed staff, and it takes a system that can manage the content and information you collect. This is where your Customer Relationship Management (CRM) software comes in handy. It not only allows you to keep track of email and phone conversations, but I included details like "Karla is having surgery on September 6, send flowers," or "Tammy is appearing on *The Today Show* on July 8, watch and comment." These notes not only kept me organized but clients really appreciated us going the extra mile to stay in touch.

Other ideas to keep in mind when building your customer service model include:

- ⚑ Solve problems and keep in touch. Rectifying a problem isn't enough, make sure you follow up and see that the client is happy in the future as well as immediately after an issue arises.

- ⚑ If the client is not a good fit, let them go with ease. The harder it is to get out of the arrangement, the quicker discontent grows.

- ⚑ Take responsibility. It's okay to say "I am sorry." Do it early and say it when it needs to said.

- ⚑ Seek feedback on the problems and make efforts to fix them. Include your customers in the loop.

Sometimes, despite trying as hard as you possibly can, you are not the right fit for your customer. If the customer doesn't choose to leave, sometimes you need to ask him or her to do so. Find a better fit for the customer, make a referral or recommendation, and move on. The customer's money is not worth the headache of trying to make a square peg fit into a round hole.

4. Setting Boundaries

Being successful in business is always about setting goals, standards, and practices for doing business. The one thing I consistently see in women is insecurity about remaining true to themselves and the policies they have set for their companies; they discount their work or product, they allow people to take advantage of their time, and they allow people to pay them late because to confront would be uncomfortable. Prepare for these scenarios before you need someone.

- Have contracts and agreements for services that clearly outline the terms and conditions of the sale.

- Have employment agreements that clearly outline the objectives in relation to the business plan. For example, "Your role needs to achieve $20,000 per month in sales."

- Become comfortable giving employees constructive criticism. Learn to ask for what you need in a way that does not make them feel threatened. If your staff do not react well to your criticisms or cannot perform as you need them, terminate them in order to move forward.

- If you take on private equity investors, defend your position as the leader, and defend your knowledge of your company — no one knows it as well as you. Just because someone is wealthy does not mean he or she has all of the answers to make you wealthy.

- In business, the only person looking out for you is you. Do not confuse friends with employees; by keeping your personal life to yourself you will prevent confusion and hurt feelings when the time comes to say something difficult or if the relationship doesn't work out.

Case Study: The Brazilian Wax Specialist

Every summer, that moment arrives when you realize that it is no longer cold and you no longer need a fur coat to keep you warm. You also realize, it will take your children about 3.5 seconds after summer is here to get their bathing suits out and dive into the nearest body of water — be it the blow-up whale pool or a scummy green puddle, they aren't picky. In response, I shed a tear, take a deep breath, and quickly call my favorite and most important esthetician, my waxer.

Now, we all want to keep things ladylike, so I am not going to go into too many details but you must know that she is the best at what she does and therefore the only one I trust with my de-woolification process! At my last appointment, as I clenched my teeth and tried to carry on a conversation, I realized that she is the perfect example of a successful woman in business.

Let me tell you why.

Her branding is fabulous. From the beginning, she has used iconic pin-up girl images as part of her brand. They are everywhere, from the website, to the walls, to the music that you listen to. She even looks like a professional version of a pin-up doll. Best of all, her personality matches the brand. She is cute, funny, and then immediately tough as nails, as any entrepreneur should be. When I asked how I would describe her to a friend, she said, without hesitation, "I am a Brazilian wax specialist" — no more, no less.

She started her business from her home eight years ago. As a result she has been able to minimize overhead expenses, invest in the highest quality waxing materials, and, most importantly, maximize profit. She gives no apology for having a home-based business; in fact, she revels in the fact that she has made it work and excelled at creating a professional space at the same time.

She has drilled down her business to offering only the services that she does best, she wastes no time on services that do not maximize her bookings and profits, and she only markets to the clientele looking for the best bikini wax out there. To maximize this, she has become an expert in the ever popular "Brazilian wax" as well as the "tiny bikini" for the more conservative segment of women visiting, including yours truly. (I know you were wondering!)

She has rules that you must read, understand, sign off on, and, if you don't follow, you will be expelled from her inner client circle, banished from that exclusive group of women, never to return.

Most entrepreneurs take every client they can with the worry they won't get another; she is consistently confident enough to tell you to bugger off, knowing that she is one of the best at what she does and will continue to have clients referred to her, regardless of the loss of your, sorry, fuzzy nether region.

She uses social media to her advantage. She has a great Facebook fan page and regularly thanks her customers for the rave reviews.

She draws boundaries. When you call for your first appointment, you are given her rules of engagement; as well as her cancellation policy, where to park, her payment terms, and her client-health policy (do not even consider darkening her door if you have the slightest cough, drip, or infection because you will be on the curb so fast, you will wonder if your unsightly fuzz was even able to follow). She is happy to remind you on your way out that not only does coming sick make her sick, but that she is an entrepreneur and has no one to cover for her when she gets your cold, and that she loses revenue as a result.

Last but not least, is that after you are given the rules, you have agreed to comply, and you have submitted to what will inevitably come next, she makes you cackle with laughter at her quick wit, her engaging charm, and her ability to make fun of herself, setting you immediately at ease — even in the most compromising of positions.

As I walk out the door, I realize that despite the fact that I just paid to have my pubic hair ripped from its roots, I am looking forward to my next appointment. Can your clients say that about you?

11

Strategizing Your Time

"I think the best thing I have is my client database — it keeps track of my clients, job bookings, organizes hours, and lots more — it helps my time management so much. I do use my Outlook calendar to keep track of business and personal activities — no separate calendars. I also still go by my old standby to-do list — always worked for me. I write everything down."

— Betsy Fein, Clutterbusters

As a mom that has decided to start and run businesses as a career, I have to admit, one of the hardest things is being able to prioritize everything that needs to be done and make sure that at the top of the list is always my family. Some days, organization of these tasks alone is overwhelming enough to bring the toughest mama to her knees in a fit of tears. Some days I feel like I have it all under control, clients are happy, tasks are completed, and money is coming in. At home, kids are fed, bathed, and happy because they have had a few hours of devoted mom time and somewhere along the way a multivitamin was thrown in. Other days are not so great. A deadline is pushed up, a task is missed, and someone is unhappy. Although I have made this mad dash at life work for a few years now, I hope to find an everlasting fix that will give me a blissfully short to-do list, and know that everything I manage is running smoothly.

As an entrepreneurial mom, every moment of available, child-free work time is used as efficiently as possible. When my daughter was four months old, I wrote the business plan for *The MOMpreneur Magazine* during every nap time and after bedtime. This meant I had to keep her on a very strict feeding and sleep schedule. Not only was this great for her, but it allowed me to have clear times to work and clear times where I would not work. It is amazing what you can get it done in the course of a nap time. To this day, I laugh when I see emails come in fast and furious between 1:00 p.m. and 3:00 p.m. every afternoon and after 7:00 p.m. Moms are my community and we are all on the same schedule of work.

Balancing time is always a juggle, there are never enough hours in the day, your children cannot have enough attention, your toilet and carpets could always use more cleaning — the list is endless. For me, the best way to combat my endlessly overwhelming to-do list is to use software that supports the projects I am involved in.

To keep my network of clients, partners, media, and people I am interested in clear, I use LinkedIn, Facebook, and Twitter. Social media are excellent tools to stay on top of what the people in your community and your competition are doing and accomplishing. In Twitter, to focus in on the target group I am most interested in at the moment, I develop lists. I have a list for media, for entrepreneurial resources, for marketing, and for mom communities. This way, I can easily jump to the group I want to follow at that moment and quickly catch up, without filtering through the 10,000 tweets from the last hour.

As social media becomes an increasingly effective tool to build my profile, I have had to implement HootSuite as a tool to manage my social media so that I can schedule my messages in advance, watch who mentions me and why, as well as monitor what my clients or prospects are doing so I can stay in the loop of their latest accomplishments.

To keep track of my email conversations with the media, prospective clients, and active accounts, I use client-relationship managers such as Salesforce, Maximizer Software, or Sage ACT! These are not always the fastest of programs, but they can chart all past conversations, I can analyze how far along a sale is, I can monitor where my sales teams are, and I can draw up reports to follow each of these items quickly.

Email management always takes twice as long as I expect it to take. For me, I have had to learn to only turn my email on at the beginning and end of each day. I try to delete as much as I possibly can at the end of each day and assign a follow-up task to the items that I cannot delete.

Managing your time and organizing your office will always be a challenge for the busy entrepreneurial mom. Recognizing it as such, allotting time to plan and organize, and forgiving yourself for becoming overwhelmed are the only keys to making it work.

1. Delegate Responsibility

"The first thing you need to do is shake the paradigm of the Monday to Friday, nine to five 'regular business hours' mindset. Once you do this, you can focus on a 'blended' day. (I don't like the words 'balance' and 'juggle' because it infers you're constantly choosing one over the other.) Make the most of your time in either your business or personal/family setting, and schedule EVERYTHING — from laundry to meetings to school activities to major project proposals. Make goals, and revisit them at least once a year — both personal ones and professional ones. Keep an active to-do list (I combine everything from 'call the orthodontist' to 'pitch magazine stories to X') and always remember to prioritize and delegate. Know what you want to spend your time on, and focus from there."

— Kathy Buckworth, author

Delegate, because there is nothing better than having an assistant that knows your business inside and out, can alert you to upcoming deadlines, and who can easily and effectively take over tasks as they begin to pile up on you.

I see so many women waste time on doing every little task themselves. As the CEO of a company, you need to assess how much your time is worth. If your business brings in $100,000 in revenue per year, and you are the only person bringing clients in, your time is worth $48 per hour. If you have any tasks that can be delegated for $10 or $15 an hour, you need to delegate!

As the CEO and visionary of your company, your main focus should be on building the company to the growth you have planned for in your business plan and on closing sales. Stop procrastinating on the important stuff by filling your time with mindless social media, email, or on mundane tasks such as packing and shipping. If you focused on the sales, you would have the cash flow to bring in an assistant to support these ventures and grow your revenue streams. If you don't have the money to do so, then either you haven't properly planned for your growth or you are not closing enough sales to sustain the growth of your business. You need to decide early on if you want a full-time job as a CEO or as a packer, shipper, and retail clerk. If it is not CEO, I suggest you get a minimum-wage job and save yourself the stress and financial risk of owning your own business.

2. Get Organized!

"Time management was difficult to program at first since I was a stay-at-home mom first and foremost. That meant sort of working on the fly and I was used to that. Gradually I learned to keep a list of what needs to be done and plan out a schedule for checking things off. Again, it doesn't have to be anything fancy. I try to keep a notebook with a running list from day to day. I'm always making new entries and I've learned the list will always be a bit on the longer side. I now embrace it. I make it a mind over matter process and tell myself that if I still have that list, I'm still in the game."

— Sheil Caldwell, RememberMyBags.com

Each entrepreneur — mother or not — needs a dedicated space for her company. If you are working from your dining room table — stop. Not only is it distracting while you are working, but it also keeps you from leaving the "office" when you want to spend some time with your kids or husband. It is hard enough leaving work at work when you have a home office, and it is virtually impossible when you have to stare at it during dinner, playtime, or date night with your husband.

Sylvia Daoust, owner of Niche Designs Inc. and a professional organizer, suggests creating three distinct zones in your office space:

Zone 1 is where it all happens. Imagine you are comfortably sitting at your computer. The phone, the printer, a calendar, your desk supplies, and your action files are all within arm's reach. Having this accessibility does *not* mean items need not be on top of your desk. Remember, your desktop is prime working space, not space for storing office supplies. When my desk is cluttered my head starts to spin and I can't focus on anything! If you don't have enough drawer storage, utilize wall space for cork or white boards and wall pockets.

Zone 2 becomes the area in which you store additional supplies, reference books, or promotional material. If you are one of the lucky ones, a closet or bookcases may provide you with the space you need for these items. Use small labeled bins or baskets to store electronic equipment, manuals, and mailing supplies.

Zone 3 is your filing cabinet to store both client files and business documents. This filing system should correspond to your electronic file names. Identify several broad categories based on your current file names (e.g., finances, marketing, personal). Label these categories based on the first word that comes into your head. When it comes time to retrieve the file, the less complicated the file name, the better.

Break down each broad category into its second-level category. These names will be specific enough for you to retrieve a document without searching through multiple folders (e.g. marketing — newsletter).

In creating these zones, you'll experience the benefits of having the things you need at your fingertips, while everything else is out of the way until you need it.

What do you recommend to stay on track for time management?

We can't change the fact that many things compete for our time week after week. Personal organization involves breaking old habits and forming new, effective ones. Free up some time by eliminating nonproductive or low-priority activities, and quickly replace them with more valuable ones.

How do you successfully manage your time?

In a word: Plan. Time spent planning is time well spent, so hit the ground running and implement these valuable tips:

- Choose three priorities that need to be completed by the end of the week. Be both specific and realistic with these three tasks.

- Divide your work day into blocks of time. When are you most productive? When is your energy level at its peak? Be sure to work on one of your top priorities during this productive block. Schedule your phone meetings and return emails *outside* of this peak time.

- By setting up systems for repetitive tasks, you can avoid wasting time reinventing the wheel. Create templates for everything from meeting agendas to proposals and agreements for clients.

❦ Keep yourself focused by sticking to the plan you set for the week. Use an egg timer to prevent yourself from spending more time on certain tasks than you planned. Don't let half of your morning slip away responding to emails or writing your daily blog.

❦ One life, one calendar. Whatever planner you choose to use, it should complement your work style. Just remember to keep all personal, family, and work-related items on *one* calendar.

❦ Procrastination comes from one of two things: You continually put off a specific task because it is too complex, or the task is something you don't like and is not your forte. A solution for the former is to break down complicated tasks into manageable time blocks. My answer for the latter is to outsource those tasks that do not build revenue or grow your business.

2.1 Little black book

Eliminate sticky notes, multiple notepads, and lonely papers strewn about the office. Find *one* notebook to keep all of the information you tend to scribble down throughout the week and label each section using tabs.

Make sure your little black book is portable. Sometimes your greatest biz ideas come to you while waiting to pick up your child at school!

2.2 Action folder

What "actions" are routine in your business? Deadlines? Follow-ups? Meeting notes? Create a folder for each of your action items, but be careful not to exceed four folders. To simplify, you may choose to have only one action folder. The paper that falls into these folders is generally items you did not have time for when they came in.

These folders can be organized in wall pockets, a literature sorter, or in your desk-filing drawer. Don't forget to label the folders clearly.

Schedule a weekly appointment in your calendar to act on all of the papers in your action folders. This is the time to make a decision; now file or toss!

2.3 Prevention is key

Don't keep shuffling papers; handle each item only once whenever possible. File it, Act on it, or Toss it (FAT).

There is no need to print everything! Save any important documents on your computer, including emails and great websites. Send e-copies of invoices and agreements to clients. There is no need to hang onto paper unnecessarily; so much information we need to access is available online.

Managing paper piles, even in our high-tech world, is an important skill for any entrepreneur. The random piles that accumulate on your desktop are a symptom of delayed decisions. Many people fear throwing away something important, when the reality is that more than 85 percent of what you do keep is never needed again. Keep papers moving through simple systems!

"I limit myself to only four photography sessions per month with the exception of newborns born at an earlier or later date if already booked with me. I often work through nap time or quiet times and during my children's bedtime routine, which my husband takes over most nights, or after the girls go to bed.

For the actual sessions I book mostly in the evenings during the week or on weekends when my husband is home. He has the ability to work from home with his work as well, so if I need to, we can arrange during the week if no other date works for my newborn sessions. I do have many late nights responding to emails and editing photos to present in client galleries, and do a lot of personal work as a method of advertising to show potential clients what I am capable of creatively with my photography skills. I really enjoy this part of the business it helps keep my spark and interest for it alive. I find it impossible to talk on the phone during the girls' waking hours, therefore I strongly encourage my clients to communicate via email."

— Amber Black, Amber Black Photography

3. The Importance of Balancing Your Life and Work

"I don't look for balance anymore, I look for harmony."

— Julie Freedman Smith, Parenting Power™

As my deadline for completing this book approached, my need for balance increased. Juggling a family, business, and the completion of a book definitely threw balance out the window.

When I look back at my career and lifestyle, it doesn't look very balanced. For the most part, I balance my family and my career, which does not leave a lot of time for me to exercise or eat right, etc. This is an ongoing project for me as I think it is for many entrepreneurial moms. What I do know is that when I do take the time to have dinner with my girlfriends, who do not own businesses and don't care how successful or not I am that year, I feel recharged for the upcoming weeks. When I turn off my BlackBerry, my phone, and my computer, and only focus on my kids for the remainder of the afternoon and evening, my playtime with them becomes more fun for them, more fulfilling for me, and builds lasting memories.

The trick, I believe, is choosing on a daily basis to make decisions around your priorities. For me, right now my priorities are building experiences and lasting memories with my children and husband, and building a fulfilling, sustainable, profitable business that includes an equitable paycheck for the amount of work I am putting in. My months go up and down in terms of how busy I am at work and with my kids, learning to follow that flow so that I can maintain my sanity is one of my biggest challenges.

Because balance is a skill I am continuing to develop, I interviewed Dr. Janet Miller, Psychologist and Associate Professor at Mount Royal University in Calgary, Alberta.

What steps do you recommend for an entrepreneurial mother to take to balance the hectic schedule of raising a family and building a business?

Balance and harmony are really personal things. We each have our own balance point, and what is in our lives is so personal, there cannot be one recipe for balance.

For myself, I love having a great life at work, and also a great life outside of work. I feel in balance when I love getting up and going to work, and when I love leaving my office and heading home. I know that I am in balance when I am sleeping well — really well — for at least six or seven hours a night of peaceful sleep. I love taking a multifaceted approach to health and wellness — considering mental, emotional, career, spiritual, physical, environmental, financial, and social aspects of myself. Ideally — I am feeding into each one of these areas — investing time, energy, and other resources to really live well in each of these facets of my life.

To help me know if I'm on track, I look for positive indicators of happiness and balance … for me, these might be:

- I am taking time to sit and eat.
- I am exercising regularly.
- I am being creative in some way … have I been making things? Staying out of the rut?
- I am patient with my kids, with my clients, and with my colleagues.
- I do not feel rushed — I am busy, but not hurried.
- I can fall asleep easily.
- I am making time to see friends.
- I laugh lots, but cry when I need to.
- I can relax and really be in the moment.
- At the end of each day I have a sense of satisfaction.

Often we look for signs of stress overload (e.g., headaches, belly-aches, being short-tempered, getting sick, drinking too much alcohol) and if we see those signs, we should take action to practice better stress-management skills. But if we're looking for "symptoms of wellness," then we're orienting ourselves to think more positively.

Good things happening (symptoms of wellness)

—— Neutral Point — not great, but not bad ——

Bad things happening (signs of stress overload,
or stress-related illness)

I encourage my clients to try to live as far above the neutral line as they can. There is more room to "fall" or "cushion" us if we hit a crisis — we're more resilient, and we're more likely to intervene early if something begins to slip.

How do you address the issue of "mom guilt"? What do you recommend for other women struggling with it?

Well, I am a mom of two lovely, happy, active, and smart children — one is four and a half, and the other just turned two. They are awesome, and like most mothers in the world, I feel incredibly grateful to know them and to be in their lives.

I am also really in love with my career — I am a psychologist — I love helping people and I love to learn. I am an associate professor at Mount Royal University, and I also have a private counseling practice and do some public speaking. I likely work 50-plus hours each week … but it doesn't really feel that way because I love what I do. I am lucky enough to be able to do some of that work during the evening hours once my kids are asleep (e.g., planning, preparation, correspondence, marking), but much of my work is still done during a regular nine to five kind of workday. As a result, my kids are both in full-time care. If my kids are safe, then I do not worry about them. Apart from safety, I need to know that they were having fun, and that they are learning things while in someone else's care … with these things in place, I found that I could let go of them, and turn my attention to my work.

I remember when my eldest first went into care at a day home. I remember lying in bed trying to count the number of hours I would be away from him … and that he would be in the care of another … and wow, it was difficult to accept the "loss." What I have learned though, for me, is that my kids benefit from being away from me, and I am a better mother when I am with them because I feed the other parts of myself when we are apart. I know this to be true for me, so that decreases my mother's guilt for sure.

Perhaps the most important thing that I've done this year that has quelled my "mother's guilt" is changing my schedule through the week to allow for one-on-one time with my kids. Because I can do a lot of my work in the evenings, I have freed up some daytime hours where I can take one of my kids out of care and spend time with him individually. At least a half day of just one-on-one time, each week, has been fantastic. Often I've signed us up for some kind of parent/child class, or we make plans to do something outdoors or something that really is only possible with one kid (because of developmental stages or interest). This "date time" has become sacred for me … and I do whatever I can to protect that time from "work invasion." I know that my kids appreciate this time … and it's nice to have the daycare support to be able to do this.

What else do I do to curb the guilt? I try to check in with myself often to see if I'm in line with my values, if I'm being the kind of parent that I want to be. My mom guilt increases when I'm distracted — when I am physically with them, but mentally not present. I try to notice if I'm in my head, or distracted, or multitasking, or saying "in a minute" a lot — "mom will be off the computer in a minute" or "in a minute honey, when I am off the phone." When I hear myself going down that road I try to guide myself back to the here-and-now, and what's really important. Self-awareness is the key. I know when I'm in tune with my kids and when I am not. I know when I am trying too hard to make up for something I'm feeling guilty about. I know when I am not saying "no" when I know that I should be, but I am feeling guilty and therefore give in instead of setting the boundary that I know would be healthier. It's tough to say "no" to them, especially after I've had a long day of working and only have a few hours with them before it's time to put them to bed … but I know that it's also essential to set those limits.

What would you recommend to entrepreneurial mothers trying to build a business and balance their family lives?

Tune into your values — what do you want to show your kids about love, life, work, and family? Is it important to you that you be with them through the day, and then fit your work in at night? Is it important that they are always with one parent or the other, or another family member? Is it important that they are together (if there is more than one child)? Is it important that they know that you love what you do? Is it important that they know about your work? See you working? Understand why you're working? Is it important that you have quality time when you are with them? Or is quantity more important? What is the balance you're aiming for? Is it important that mothers and children have their own friends or social circles? Is it important that kids get the chance to make friends on their own (rather than be friends with the children of our friends)? Is it important to have cross-cultural experiences?

When you can't have the ideal … it can be hard. For example, you might wish to be a stay-at-home parent, but reality might dictate that you go to work and have to leave your kids … what can you change about this? Your work? Your attitude? Your balance? You might prefer for your kids to be with family when they are young, but you might not have family nearby … what is workable?

I'm not just working because I have to (although I do need to make a living); I work because I love to. I'm not just parenting because I have to … I'm with my kids because I love being with them.

It's all out of love … and I know my kids get this about me. They see me leave to go to work (which is sometimes really hard on them), but then they see me come back. I think this helps to build trust and security. They also get to meet lots of other people in their day, they are exposed to other caring people and they learn and grow, and we have lots to talk about and share. All of this is congruent with my values — I want my kids to be social, curious, active, and confident … and I want us to have our own identities, as well as our collective identity.

3.1 Tuning into Your Body

Understanding that there really is no such thing as balance is easy to understand, whereas finding day-to-day harmony can be extremely difficult. It has taken me a lot of years, and having children, to find out how to tune back into my body when things are out of whack and realign.

When I get really stressed about work; whether it is dealing with a dispute, however large or small; coping with too many close deadlines; or dealing with relationship dynamics of partners, clients, or board members, I can now take time to put things back into perspective. For me, stopping what I am doing, spending time with my kids with the phone and TV turned off, and tuning out the stress of work helps me bring my priorities back into alignment. Don't get me wrong, there are times when I find this exercise challenging, but as soon as I do it life becomes easier.

It was not always this way. When I speak about my business disaster, I remember that my stress levels were through the roof. My blood pressure was regularly 180/110, I had frequent migraines, and I rarely slept through the night. I was constantly checking the bank account, worrying about the next incoming check, the next outgoing payroll — it was a circus. I went through a bottle of TUMS every week and my relationship with my fiancé (now husband) was always put in second place.

It took losing everything to realize that it just wasn't worth it. Although humiliating, walking into a bankruptcy trustee's office and waving the white flag was one of my most freeing moments. I was 26 years old, newly married, and almost half a million dollars in debt. I had tried, accomplished great things, and failed. It was over. As soon as I signed on the dotted line, I felt reborn; I could start fresh, begin again, and try something new. This would lead to me building the only national women's business magazine in Canada by the age of 28 and with a 16-month-old girl in tow. I was able to accomplish my financial goals, my career goals, but more important than anything else, I was able to be the mom that I wanted to be, the mom my mom taught me to be. I wanted to be my child's primary caregiver as well as do something with my career that challenged me.

This experience, although easily one of the toughest times of my life, prepared me to go into new opportunities with the experience to be a leader in business, to not be afraid to make difficult choices, and to know when to say something is wrong or to pull the plug, whether that is overspending, acknowledging I have made a mistake, or walking away when it is no longer worth it. These decisions and conversations with stakeholders are never easy, but it is far easier than rebuilding a relationship, rebuilding your health, or rebuilding your financial well-being.

At this point in my book, my editor suggested I give you a few more comments on balance. To be honest, it is not a skill at which I excel. I know I need to take time to exercise, to have weekly dates with my husband, and to have some time to myself — but this week, this month actually, it is just not happening. What I have realized is that, just like making sure my kids get enough fruits and vegetables, I need to look at my overall balance over the course of a week or a month. There will just be times in my life where I will not have time to eat right, exercise, spend some time by myself, and gaze into my husband's eyes. What I try to remember is that when I do, I feel much, much better about the track that I am on, and I find clarity in the direction I am going and the decisions I have to make.

If I see myself getting more stressed, looking for something to throw at my husband, or getting angry at my kids for inconsequential things, it is a huge indicator to me that I need to take some time and reassess what I need to do to bring a little balance back in. Here are some things I do to regain perspective:

- If things are really stressful, nothing puts things into better perspective than turning off my phones, my computers, and all extra noise and getting on the floor and playing with my kids. I know you are going to say that you do this a million times a day anyway, and I do too, but if you think about it, how often do you really try to focus only on them, turning all outside distractions off, and only enjoy them in those moments? That focused time does not always happen as often as it should for us working moms.

- I have a monthly girls' night out with two women who are exactly the opposite of entrepreneurial and make me laugh until I pee my pants, consistently. We stay up too late, eat crazy spicy food, and tell stories that would make a hooker blush!

- I read a really great novel. One of my biggest passions has always been reading. I will read anything and everything. It took a long time to figure out that watching TV winds me up and reading relaxes me; once I did realize this, I got rid of the TV in my bedroom. I now go through at least a book a week and have gotten to know my online library service *very* well.

❦ I need to go to sleep by 10:00 p.m. My kids are up by 5:00 a.m. For me to function at my best, I need to have at least seven hours of sleep. Figure out what amount of rest works for you and then stick to it.

❦ I need to have sex a couple of times a week (*usually* with my husband — just kidding — ha!). I know this is odd to mention in a business book, but we are talking balance here. Having sex with my husband makes me feel more emotionally connected to him and less likely to think of the heaviest object I can throw when he annoys me!

❦ Finally, I am a loner. I know not everyone is, but this is my book and my list. Having a couple of hours to myself can make the difference between a crappy week and blissful one for me. It doesn't matter what I do; having a chunk of time where I am not responsible for anyone but myself feels like crazy, self-indulgent bliss.

12

Your Exit Strategy

Of the 150 women I have interviewed for this book, about 25 percent either chose to leave a business or declared bankruptcy as a result of a poorly performing business. Although this is not something that anyone likes to discuss, the experiences gained during such occurrences can be used as an important learning tool for women either thinking of starting a business or women who are already embedded within one. Some of the lessons learned include:

- Mission drift: If you decide to start adding to your core-revenue streams, make sure they are profitable additions. Of the women who have left a business, many walked away because they had begun focusing too much time outside of their main mission and had lost focus and perspective.

- Overspending on equipment. Do not get the best and the most beautiful equipment. Assess what you can afford, and have money left over for a war chest. You will need it.

- Running a failing business becomes like an addict getting a fix, except your fix is money. You begin to think of only money, where it will come from, how you can get it, and what you will do to get it. Once you are there, you are done.

❧ Don't be afraid to leave a failing business. It may just be the dress rehearsal for your next amazing opportunity. You don't lose the experience and knowledge you have gained, you just lose the stress of having gone down the wrong path.

Recognizing that your business is not your "baby" and learning to see it only as an outlet for your creativity and a vehicle for income keeps things in perspective. If you are able to build a business that thrives and survives its first ten years, then you have accomplished something many haven't been able to do.

Knowing what your long-term plan for yourself in the business is can sometimes be difficult to decide, but an exit strategy is something every entrepreneur needs to have. For many, the strategy is to sell their creation to the highest bidder and retire happy. From experience, I know once you are an entrepreneur, you are an entrepreneur for life. Others enjoy their work so much that they have created a business that becomes a lifestyle and a structure for living their day-to-day experiences.

As you plan your future around your business and plan your exit strategies (succession planning), you have options to consider:

❧ Building your business to pass on to your children — or at least the smart child of the bunch — that is, only if the children want it.

❧ Selling your business to an outside party.

❧ Liquidating your business or selling off your assets when the time comes. This would be your only option if you have not put the proper systems in place to sell.

1. Selling Your Business

"Nobody gets rich running their business; they get rich selling their business."

Kim Lavine, entrepreneur and author

Deciding to leave *The MOMpreneur Magazine* was one of the hardest decisions I have ever had to make. My original goal in building that company was to stay home with my kids while they were young and be a mom that was there at the end of every school day and available when they needed me. *The MOMpreneur Magazine* grew quickly. With growth and private equity come board members with their own agendas — always to make money, and there is nothing wrong with that. All of a sudden, I had to put my family at the bottom of the list in order to meet the needs of the company, especially during the recession. By December of 2009, I had had enough and I decided to leave.

Making that decision was difficult. It was hard to leave my business that had grown into something so special, and after, it was hard to see it change from what I had hoped it would become. What wasn't hard was leaving behind a stressful situation to spend more time with my family. No matter how I look at it, it was the right choice — financially, emotionally, and in terms of my career — and I haven't looked back.

If your exit strategy is to sell your company and enjoy the fruits of your labor, you need to build a company that has systems and procedures in place so that it doesn't rely on you to survive. If you were hit by a bus tomorrow, your business plan and team need to be able to carry on the business and go forward. This is what a salable business has to offer.

Here is a checklist for your exit strategy planning that is taken from *Finance & Grow Your New Business: Get a Grip on the Money*, by Angie Mohr, CA, CMA (Self-Counsel Press, 2008):

- I know what my retirement goals are.
- I have determined the time frame in which I want to retire.
- I have looked into the possibility of passing the business on to my heirs.
- I have considered the possibility of selling the business to an employee.
- I have looked into the opportunities for selling the business to an outside party.
- I have assessed the benefits and costs of simply liquidating the company.
- I have met with my accountant to prepare for the eventual sale of my business.

When planning to sell your business, you need to have the following components ready to go:

- What is your business worth? A professional valuation can be extremely costly but you can determine a value for your business using simple standard formulas. For the most part, I find entrepreneurs grossly overvalue their businesses. Start by figuring out your earnings before interest, taxes, depreciation, and amortization (EBITDA), and then subtract your minimum amount of new capital expenditures required each year. From there, you need to consider some of the intangible items such as website traffic, whether or not you have a broad stream of regularly purchasing clients, and how large and comprehensive your client database is.

🛒 Every industry has a multiple or the amount you multiply your EBITDA by in order to find a value. This multiple can be anywhere from three to eight times your EBITDA. This multiple can be influenced by interest rates as well as competitors in the market place. Find a broker who can help you establish a proper valuation with your accountant and help you market your business to the right buyers.

🛒 Once you have a buyer, prepare to negotiate, be open to different deal structures, and have a lawyer help you take the right option.

🛒 Prepare for due diligence. The due diligence process on the part of the buyer can be extraordinarily time intensive and will probably make you want to pull your hair out before it is done. Be prepared for the buyer to want to review all financials, contracts, client lists, and intellectual property. The buyer will also want to do background checks and interview all key officers of the company and decide whether or not to keep them or move forward with their own team.

🛒 Transition planning: Potentially you will need to train the new buyer, transition the employees to the leadership of the new buyer, and keep clients happy during this transition.

🛒 Decide whether you want to start a new business, invest in others, write a substantial check to a charity, or live on the beach for the rest of your days. This last task is my favorite!

2. The Power of Choice — Going Forward

As I travel around the country, speaking to women who have chosen to go down the entrepreneurial mother's path, I inevitably get asked, "If statistics have shown more than 80 percent of businesses do not survive their first year, let alone their fifth year, why does anyone do it?" My answer is this: Of all of the women I have worked with, I have hoped that my advice has helped them overcome the risk of having to walk away their first year, and for the most part it has. What I see more often than not, is that women who have started a business now have a taste for what it truly can be when they have taken control of their careers in order to be more engaged in every aspect of their family's life. They have envisioned success, whatever that means to them, and are now not willing to settle for anything less.

Of all of the women I interviewed for this book, not one of them said that she had would not do it again, no matter if she had been successful or if she had had a couple of "dress rehearsals" for her next big business. Being a mother can be one of the most challenging yet exhilarating times in a woman's life, and being an entrepreneur comes close to matching that adventure.

I hope that with this book you have learned some of the strategies that will help you go forward with ease, exhilaration, and the joy of adventure. I continue to look for your stories as you move towards greatness and hear what is working for you and what didn't.

Our current economic climate is going to be the catalyst for a new economic revolution for women in business. It is a time for businesses that are technologically oriented, tapped into large communities through social media, and that break the old rules of having offices, boardrooms, and corporate culture. I encourage you to challenge anyone who tells you that those antiquated models are the way of the future for the entrepreneurial mom.

When all else fails, go with your gut: Mothers were not built to break.

Appendix I: Your Toolkit

Once you have children, your days of grabbing your purse and jumping into your car are gone. The same goes for becoming an entrepreneurial mom, as your diaper bag/toolkit suddenly becomes more cumbersome. The following are the essentials tools every woman needs to have or understand:

- **Understand and implement a remote browser:** I don't care if you have built yourself the most beautiful office available: Sometimes you just need to get away from your home, your children, your husband, whoever, and relocate. For me, I do my best writing in bed. During the eight short weeks of summer that my city experiences, I like to work outside or at least by a sunny window instead of my cozy but dark basement office. Mostly though, when I am feeling overwhelmed and have a to-do list the length of my husband's leg, I put the kids to bed and leave the house. A remote browser allows me to log into my computer from anywhere in the world as long as I have access to the Internet.

  - My favorite software is GoToMyPC.com. It is simple, inexpensive, and allows me easy access to all of my files and any work I do. It is just like I am working on my desktop in my office.

- 🛒 **Smartphone:** Most of us already have one of these, but every so often I come across a sweet little Luddite insisting her plain old cell phone is just fine. In today's world, missing an email can mean the loss of a major sale. It also allows us to send reminders, questions, or last minute emails to virtual assistants, clients, or spouses, saving countless trips to the computer. I also appreciate the new apps (applications) that not only allow you to tweet and post Facebook messages, but the apps and games for your children are priceless.

- 🛒 **Customer Relationship Management (CRM) software:** This tool is essential for any business. The best CRMs will track new leads, client accounts, and order histories, as well as special notes about each history that makes you sound knowledgeable about clients even if you haven't spoken to them in three years. Some programs also allow you to send out large amounts of email newsletters to all clients, stakeholders, and potential leads and track their efficacy. Some of my favorites include Salesforce.com, ACT.com, and Maximizer Software. Most software providers have a 30-day free trial so you can get to know the programs before committing.

- 🛒 **Website:** Having a strong website is pretty much a no-brainer at this point, but have you thought about adding an online newsletter? Does your website track your online traffic, does it have a call to action, can you update it yourself, and is it current? Making a website is not just about making something that tells people how to get hold of you, it becomes a tool to engage your target market and build a community. Simple add-ons such as a link to follow you on Twitter and Facebook, or a sign-up button for your online newsletter, are essential to communicating with your future clients. Make sure your sign-up button is in the top right-hand corner — one of the most visited areas by your reader's eye.

- 🛒 **Understand important legal agreements:** It doesn't take an entrepreneur long to recognize her need to have a basic understanding of a lot of areas of business law. If you are hiring staff as employees, you need to understand human rights laws, tax laws, and employment standards in your area. If you are discussing your invention or prototype with a potential buyer or client, you need to have a non-disclosure agreement to protect your idea. If you want to sell your business, take on a partner, give a loan, get a loan, or apply a lien, you need to have a resource for understanding these components of the law quickly and easily.

❦ **Understand mark-ups and pricing structures:** If you plan to manufacture a product, you need to understand the basic concept of keystone. If your product costs you $10 to make per unit or your wholesale unit cost is $10, your retail price if you have "keystone" is $20. Most retailers will not buy your product unless it is reasonable to double the wholesale cost of your unit. You have to be able to calculate how much it will cost you to make one of your products. If you can't figure this out, find an accountant to help. You then need to poll a number of knowledgeable buyers to see if your price point is reasonable. If you go to mass market, you may need to negotiate the unit price down even further based on volumes. This is where it becomes essential that you understand your financials, your costs to make a unit, and that you have analyzed and negotiated every cost to make it as cost-effective as possible.

- To get a feel for where your pricing should be as a service provider, you need to do a comparative analysis of what others in your field are charging for the same services. Do not underprice your service because you are just starting out and you need to close clients. Focus on your target market, do a great job, go the extra mile, charge for what you are worth, and then watch as the referrals roll in.

❦ **Line sheets:** I became very familiar with line sheets when I started a company by the name of Wild Octopus, a sales representation company for women who manufacture juvenile products for North American markets. Each line that we carried had to have a line sheet, a one page summary of the features of the products, images of the products on their own, with models, and price points. It was like a quick cheat sheet for a buyer who wanted more information at a glance. I have since used this model in other businesses. When I wanted to close a potential client, I often attached a quick line sheet of targets I felt I could achieve for them in a more creative and visual medium that supported my text-based proposal. (When selling one business, I did a line sheet with a quick overview of the key selling features and the potential for moving forward.)

❦ **Database of articles on your area of expertise and a short bio:** Every woman starting her own business needs to become the expert in her own field. Whether your field is manufacturing gift baskets, professional organization, or consulting on search engine optimization, you need to be able to speak and write intelligently about that topic from a variety of different angles. An area of marketing that is often overlooked is article marketing. Many websites, newsletters, and media outlets are looking for articles to publish to educate their readers, populate their sites with fresh content, or to fill regular newsletters with quality content.

Research which outlets in your target market regularly publish articles and ask to submit some writing samples. Make sure your articles are similar in length to those that are regularly published on that site and follow the writing style guides laid out by that outlet. Follow every article with a short bio about you, make sure you focus on driving traffic to your website, signing people up to your online newsletter, and letting them approach you for business. To see more of my articles as examples, go to www.entrepreneurialmombook.com.

- **Photos:** Finally, most entrepreneurs who are in business understand the need for really great photos of their products or some sort of photo of their service, but many disregard the need for a really great photo of themselves. This is essential, and it should be on your website, your Twitter page, your Facebook page, and included in your bios when marketing yourself by writing articles. You should look attractive and approachable. I learned quickly while owning a magazine that the magazines that sold the most were those that showed women who were attractive, looked into the camera, and smiled showing teeth — yes, showing their teeth. Do what you need to do to have a few great shots in your arsenal. That may mean hiring a stylist and a makeup artist, and having your photographer touch up your photos so the last week of all-nighters with your flu-ish two-year-old doesn't make you look like the shrew in your children's nursery rhymes!

Appendix II: Resources

The Entrepreneurial Mom's Two-Day Seminar

Are you ready to take your business to the next level, to learn how to get your business in front of the media, and to secure private investment for your business's growth? Then join the author for a two-day, kid-free seminar. See Kathryn and other experts explain how they made their businesses work and show you how to do it. Go to www.entrepreneurialmombook.com for schedules and locations.

The Entrepreneurial Mom's TeleCoaching Program

If you would like to have one-on-one coaching with Kathryn and learn how to build your business immediately, access the media, incorporate private equity, and launch your business now, go to www.entrepreneurialmombook.com for more information.